Essential
Bali
and Jakarta

by
CHRISTINE OSBORNE

Christine Osborne is a travel writer with a
special interest in the East. She has travelled
widely in the Middle East, North Africa and
Southeast Asia. Among the books she has
written is the *Essential Guide to Thailand*, and
her photographs appear in leading
publications.

KU-207-102

Produced by AA Publishing

2

Written by Christine Osborne
Peace and Quiet section
by Paul Sterry
Original photography
by Christine Osborne

Reprinted December 1995
Revised second edition January 1995
First published January 1991

Edited, designed and produced by
AA Publishing.
© The Automobile Association 1995.
Maps © The Automobile Association
1995.

Distributed in the United Kingdom
by AA Publishing, Norfolk House,
Priestley Road, Basingstoke,
Hampshire, RG24 9NY.

A CIP catalogue record for this book
is available from the British Library.

ISBN 0 7495 0922 8

Published by AA Publishing, a
trading name of Automobile
Association Developments Limited,
whose registered office is Norfolk
House, Priestley Road, Basingstoke,
Hampshire, RG24 9NY.
Registered number 1878835.

Colour separation: Mullis Morgan
Ltd, London.

Printed by: Printers Trento, S.R.L.,
Italy

*Front cover picture: Traditional
Dance*

This book employs a simple
rating system to help choose
which places to visit:

| ✓ | 'top ten' |

♦♦♦   do not miss
♦♦   see if you can
♦   worth seeing if you
      have time

A green and pleasant land: Indonesia is rich with vegetation

INTRODUCTION TO INDONESIA

Nowhere in the world offers such diverse and fascinating contrasts as the island Republic of Indonesia. Landscape ranges from coral atolls to volcanoes stretching across the backbone of Sumatra, Java, Bali and other islands in the east. Of 300 volcanoes, 128 are active, more than half of which have erupted. More than 300 known ethnic groups, each with its own culture and speaking some 200 distinct languages, inhabit the 13,677 islands in the archipelago. It would take you 38 years of island-hopping to visit each one! Covering a land area of 741,000 square miles (nearly 2 million sq km) the archipelago extends for 3,180 miles (5,120km), roughly the distance between New York and San Francisco. Astride the equator, Indonesia is covered with lush vegetation – forests, coconut palms and jungle exotica, especially orchids.

No fewer than 15,000 tropical species are recorded. This humid, green habitat is home for many rare animals, including the Java tiger, Komodo dragon and the magnificent birds of paradise (see **Peace and Quiet** pages 77–86).

Indonesia's History

Indonesia's history is like a many-tiered cake with successive migrations and invasions covering the ethnic base. When Hindus from India reached the archipelago about 2,000 years ago, they found an indigenous people, animists (spirit-worshippers), with a distinctive culture. The *Bali Aga*, who still live in separate communities in Bali, are descendants of original inhabitants (see pages 70 and 71). The first Hindu societies were swallowed up by a powerful Hindu empire, the Sriwijaya, which rose to prominence in southern Sumatra in the 7th century AD and whose influence extended

INTRODUCTION TO INDONESIA

Symbols of two religions side by side: Jakarta's mosque and cathedral

over much of the Indian Ocean for some 500 years. Buddhism too had reached Indonesia, most impressively represented by the spectacular 8th-century Buddhist temple at Borobodur on Java.

Of great importance in Indonesian history was the 14th-century Hindu kingdom of Majapahit in East Java, under which efforts were made to unify the islands and cultures of Indonesia. Islam was the next invader, largely supplanting Hinduism and Buddhism by the end of the 14th century. European influence began in the 16th century with the arrival of Portuguese traders, later expelled by the British and then the Dutch. The Dutch colonial role began with the establishment of a trading post in Jakarta in 1602. The Japanese occupied Indonesia from 1942 to 1945. Independence was proclaimed in 1945 and eventually recognised by the Netherlands in 1949.

From 1949 to 1965, under President Soekarno, Indonesia's progress was often chaotic and bloody. Thousands were slaughtered following the abortive Communist coup in 1965. Indonesia has enjoyed peace and increasing prosperity under President Suharto, a former military chief nominated by the Provisional People's Consultative Assembly in 1967.

Government

Indonesia pursues a form of democratic government based on the philosophy of *Pancasila* (the Five Basic Principles). These are: belief in one God, righteousness and moral humanity, democracy, social justice and unity. The national motto is 'Unity through Diversity'. Central government, the People's Consultative Assembly, determines federal policies from Jakarta. The president who holds wide executive powers.

People and Religion

The fifth most densely populated country in the world – about 170 millions – Indonesia is predominantly Muslim. About 87 per cent of people follow orthodox Islam; 7 per cent are Christian; 3 per cent are Hindu or Buddhist and the remaining tribes are animists. About 65 per cent of the total population lives on the island of Java. Jakarta, the Indonesian capital, has a two-thirds Muslim population. The Balinese follow local Balinese-Hinduism. The national language is *Bahasa Indonesia* (Indonesian), but English is understood in most larger towns.

Economy

Despite the growth of tourism and other industries in Bali, village life is still in evidence

Indonesia is rich in natural resources, but while 90 per cent of the population is engaged in agriculture, oil and gas contribute 70 per cent of total earnings. A member of OPEC, Indonesia is the eleventh major oil-producer in the world.

Besides oil and liquefied natural gas, minerals, forestry products, coffee and tea make major contributions to export earnings. Progress in light industry and manufactured goods makes Indonesia an attractive emerging market for foreign investors. Local plants assemble various types of vehicles under foreign licence. The Indonesian Aircraft Industry produces two types of fixed wing aircraft and helicopters. Tourism is gaining prominence as a foreign exchange earner. At present it is only fully exploited in places such as Bali; the extension of tourism to other areas is the country's greatest potential source of revenue.

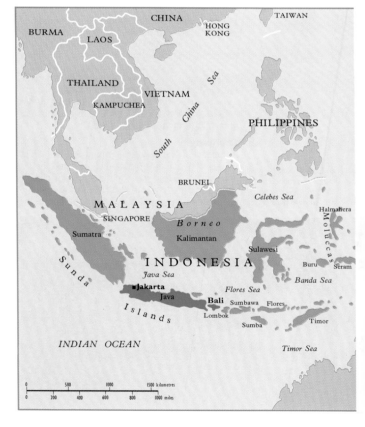

BACKGROUND TO BALI

Writers, artists and travellers have lavished praise on Bali, the jewel-like island planted in the navel of the Indonesian archipelago. Its beautiful women and exotic culture caused many an ancient mariner to jump ship. Although Hindu beliefs reached the island by the 10th–11th centuries, it remained cut off from the outside world until a Dutch invasion in 1906.

A million tourists a year are predicted for Bali by the late 1990s. Despite local hawkers and loud Australians, most newcomers are enchanted by the lush, green isle. People who knew Bali before the tourist boom find many changes but close scrutiny reveals they are superficial. Balinese culture has met Western lifestyle head-on, but instead of being swamped, it has survived.

Behind this miracle are deep religious convictions and close family ties. Balinese beachboys may wear lycra board-shorts and ride Japanese motorbikes, but at heart they are Balinese. Evidence of local resilience is a poignant ceremony each evening in Kuta, the town most affected by tourism. On Bemo Corner – the busiest intersection in Bali – a priest leads prayers amid noise, pollution and curious onlookers. Somehow the Balinese have managed to master the difficult trick of being 'raped', while retaining their dignity.

Geography and Land-use

Lying eight degrees south of the equator off East Java, Bali is the first in a string of islands known as Nusa Tengarra. It has a land area of 2,170 square miles (5,620 sq km) and measures 87 by 50 miles (140 by 80km): small enough to cycle round. Central Bali consists of considerable mountain thrusts and active volcanoes. Smoking gently, Gunung Agung – the 'Mother of Mountains' – is 10,306 feet (3,142m). When it

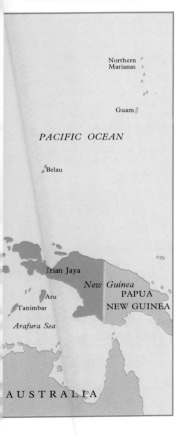

Northern Marianas

Guam

PACIFIC OCEAN

Belau

Irian Jaya

New Guinea

PAPUA NEW GUINEA

Aru

Tanimbar

Arafura Sea

AUSTRALIA

BACKGROUND TO BALI

erupted in 1963, lava flowed down to the sea with terrible loss of life. Bali's fertile soil and high rainfall make it one of the most productive rice-growing areas in Indonesia. Rising in steps to the sky, the ingeniously irrigated paddy-fields are a masterpiece of ancient engineering. Tabanan and Gianyar are the richest farming areas. There is no special rice-growing season: plants are being sown in one field next to another where rice is being cut. The yield is two, sometimes three crops a year although farming methods remain primitive. Buffalo and cows are used for ploughing, threshing is done by hand. Scarecrows, fluttering ribbons and children playing truant frighten birds away from the ripening grain. Each farm has a small shrine

Seaweed gatherers' haul from the Nusa Lembongan lagoon

where offerings are made to ensure a bountiful harvest. Coffee and exotic fruits are grown on the moist mountain slopes. Copra is important on the coast. There are fledgling shrimp-breeding farms near Negara and Benoa.

On the drier north coast cattle are raised for export. Tobacco, kapok and corn are grown and grapes flourish. In the Badung Straits off Klungkung, the island of Nusa Penida is very dry. Occupations are cattle-raising and farming corn and cashew-nuts. The well aerated lagoons off Nusa Lembongan are ideal for seaweed cultivation. Bali teems with fish, but the Balinese are farmers, not fishermen. Painting, sculpting and weaving are important cottage industries. Tourism is a big money-spinner, but most earnings bypass Bali to enrich investors from Jakarta and Surabaya.

History

Bali probably had a Stone Age culture but the earliest records date only from engravings of the 9th century AD. Hindu influence began spreading from Java in the 11th century: the rock-cut tombs of Gunung Kawi in Gianyar district date from this time. The island remained semi-independent until the Pejeng rulers clashed with the Majapahit dynasty (see page 6) in 1343. Gajah Mada, the illustrious Majapahit minister after whom hundreds of Indonesian streets are named, brought the island back under Javanese control. This status quo was maintained during 200 years' rule of the Gelgel dynasty based near present-day Klungkung.

Weakened by the Muslim invasion in the 15th century, the Majapahit dynasty collapsed. There followed a mass exodus of Javanese intelligentsia to Bali – artists, sculptors, scholars and priests taking sacred Hindu texts. Among them was the High Priest Nirartha who introduced new ideas into Bali's already eclectic brand of Hinduism and spirit worship.

Scouring the East Indies for spices, the Dutch reached Bali in 1597. The island was then at the peak of its artistic prosperity, but as it grew rice, not cloves and peppers, the Dutch were not interested and sailed away.

When the Gelgel dynasty began to break up, in the 19th century, Dutch ships reappeared off the outer reefs. Vague salvage rights to a shipwreck were used as a pretext to land Dutch forces on the north coast of Bali. When a second ship foundered off Sanur in 1904, the Dutch demanded damages of 3,000 silver dollars from the Raja of Badung. When he refused to kowtow, they landed and marched on Denpasar. On 20 September 1906, outnumbered but still refusing to surrender, the three princes of Badung led the entire royal family in a ritual *puputan* or mass suicide. Four thousand were killed.

Hearing the news, the kingdoms of Gianyar and Karangasem capitulated. But in Tabanan the raja also committed suicide and the last royal family of Klungkung also opted bravely for a *puputan*. Bali like the rest of Indonesia became part of the Netherlands East Indies.

Dutch rule from Singaraja was low-key as well as short-lived. Bali remained under Japanese occupation throughout World War II and independence for Indonesia was only recognised by The Hague in 1949.

Following the attempted coup in 1965, thousands of Communists, including many in Bali, were slaughtered. Today the island makes local decisions at district level, but major policies come from central government in Jakarta.

The People

Bali has a population of around three million. They are generally small-framed people with delicate features and considerable grace. Balinese women are beautiful, fragile creatures with Pepsodent smiles and doe-like eyes. They

BACKGROUND TO BALI

have always been in demand as foreign brides. Both sexes have a sense of humour, are warm and extremely hospitable towards strangers. Honesty is another trait. Until tourism attracted miscreants from other islands, you could leave things anywhere without risk. Politeness comes naturally to the Balinese. While doubtless shocked by Western ways, they are too courteous to comment. Extraordinarily creative, they are also deeply religious. Religion and the arts combine in a natural, never-ending pageant.

Religion

Like Islam elsewhere in Muslim Indonesia, Hinduism permeates every aspect of Balinese lives. Balinese-Hinduism is the islanders' own interpretation of ancient Hinduism, an exotic schism involving considerable spirit worship. While much of the culture is based on the main Hindu deities - Vishnu, Shiva and Brahma – the Balinese have their own gods: Sun-Gods, Moon-Gods, Turtle Gods and scores of other mythical creatures. Evil spirits inhabit the sea. The Balinese are terrified of going out too far and few can swim. Instead they worship the mountains believed to be the dwelling places of the gods. And the gods and spirits must constantly be appeased. As well as in the temples, every house has a shrine where offerings are made of small palm-leaf baskets containing flowers, rice, salt, chilli and burning incense. Balinese-Hinduism is directed at maintaining a balance between

opposing forces: good and evil, hot and cold, etc. Harmony is essential. People are, however, exceptionally superstitious and in reality, spirits dominate their psyche. Nothing important is arranged without consulting a priest who determines the most auspicious date.

Temples

Bali has more temples, or *pura*, than anywhere in the world. Every village has several and an estimate of the total might be 20,000. *Pura* is Sanskrit, meaning a space surrounded by a wall. Each *pura* is aligned towards the mountains; the holiest shrines are found at this end of the courtyard. The most important temple, the *pura puseh*, is dedicated to the village founders; *pura desa*, in the centre of the village, is for spirits protecting the people in everyday life. In the direction of the sea is the *pura dalem*, or Temple of the Dead. Temples are basically similar. They consist of multiple courtyards entered through an elaborate gateway flanked by fearsome guardians. The outer courtyard with the alarm drum, or *kulkul*, is used for meetings. It is also used for preparing food on the occasion of a festival. The inner courtyard is likewise entered through a narrow gate up a flight of steps also guarded by mythical creatures or small, protective shrines. Inside are the tall, multi-roofed towers, or *merus*, and smaller stone shrines dedicated to various gods. An important temple has a throne associated with Surya, the Balinese Sun-God. A soaring

Gifts of fruit are taken as offerings for temple celebrations

piece of sculpture, it depicts the world's three cosmic levels. Serpents, turtles and *garudas* – winged bird-men – are among an elaborate assemblage of creatures. Balinese have no objection to your visiting their temples, but custom decrees you wear a sash (see page 103). A temple is a quiet place until the occasion of its *odalan*, or 'birthday'. Every temple celebrates this feast in honour of its consecration once every 210 days on the Balinese calendar. *Odalan* is greatly anticipated by the villagers and prayers, feasting and entertainment last for three days, a rare occasion to stay up late.

A procession with women bearing vast pyramids of fruit, cakes and flowers on their heads is one of the sights of Bali, as they proudly walk like mannequins, in single file to the temple. Inside, their offerings are blessed by the priest sprinkling holy water on them. They are placed in a row as part of the general decoration and the women dance the slow *pendet*. Enlivened by the music of a *gamelan* (see page 94–5), this scene in the sacred innermost countryard may not be accessible to visitors. In the temple precincts, however, are shadow-plays, dance-dramas, foodstalls and probably a cockfight. The Balinese are very gracious about tourists attending a temple festival but do not be too pushy and do not use a camera flash.

With so many temples, it is not hard to find one having a festival. So colourful a spectacle is it, that the Bali Government Tourism Office publishes a special calendar. Also including other important holidays, it may be obtained free from their offices (see **Directory** page 123).

BACKGROUND TO BALI

Cremation

The elaborate ceremony surrounding a cremation has become a tourist attraction. Indeed, you can have a 'cremation tour' – the genuine event. Some tourists are surprised at the jubilation, but a local funeral is a happy occasion. There are no tears when someone dies on Bali. The Balinese believe a person consists of three bodies: physical, cerebral and spiritual. The body is the temple of the soul and only when it is destroyed is the cycle complete. It is a sacred duty falling on every Balinese to give the soul of a parent, or relative, a suitable send-off.

A poor family may keep a corpse for years until they can afford a proper funeral. It is buried in a coffin and the fluids drained off to prevent decomposition. When a high-caste person dies, and is to be cremated, the 'poor body' is then exhumed to participate in the funeral of the wealthy person. When a surviving member of the royal family died recently, some 500 corpses were cremated at the same time. A Brahman priest, on the other hand, may not be buried and he is cremated quickly. Aware of the cost involved, a rich man saves for his cremation – and it is expensive. Costs include the priest's fee, food and entertainment as well as a bill for the ornate ceremonial towers and sarcophagi built by village artisans.

When the family can afford it, they retrieve the remains of their relative on a date set by the priest. Covered with white cloths, the corpse is placed on a decorated bier outside the

To baffle the soul of the dead, a funeral bier is spun in circles

house. Ritual accessories are laid on the platform. Among these are a rice-filled coconut, symbolising the heart, and a small eggshell lamp representing the soul. Important rites revolve around two effigies of the soul: one a silhouette made from a palm-leaf, the other made from a thin tablet of sandalwood. The deceased's name is attached to each effigy, or *adegam*.

On the eve of the cremation, huge quantities of food arrive. Men sit up all night preparing rice, *lawar* (raw meat and blood) and other dishes for the feast, shared between hundreds. On the great day, women dress in their best including a black headscarf. Commercialism being what it is on Bali, a rich household may provide black T-shirts for male mourners and members of the *gamelan*. Then what seems a sober ceremony explodes into life.

Urged on by the *gamelan*, dozens of men rush to transport the corpse to the cremation site. Jogging through the rice-paddies, the procession is one of the most fantastic sights in Southeast Asia. It is led by women carrying offerings. Bearers follow with huge cremation towers, 8-10 tiers high, made of bamboo, tinsel, cloth, mirrors and flowers. There may be as many as 50 to 80 if the deceased was a Brahman. In the middle, on a richly gilded bier, rides the corpse. A priest hangs on, half-way up the tower, throwing holy water over the crowd. An enormous effigy of Bhoma – Son of the Earth – wild, winged and displaying huge fangs, covers the base of each tower. Every 50 metres, the procession halts, and bearers carrying the corpse spin around wildly with the priest hanging on grimly. The method in this apparent madness is to confuse the soul so that it cannot find its way back to the house. Round and round it is spun on the men's shoulders. Laughing and falling over, they all try to lend a hand to show loyalty to the deceased. Huge sarcophagi are also carried to the cremation site. Caste (see page 103) dictates their shape: a white bull (or cow) for a Brahman, a winged lion for a Satria, and a mythical creature, half-elephant, half-fish, for a Sudra. At the cremation site, these are placed above the corpse under a canopy of white cloth. Immediate relatives slash the shrouds exposing the corpse. Reciting final prayers, the priest smashes pots of holy water on the ground around the funeral pyre. The *adegams* are placed on the chest and old Chinese coins are scattered over the body (symbolic of a ransom to Yama, a deity of death).

The tower, sarcophagus and pavilion are now set alight. As matches are considered unclean, a blow torch is used on the skull and feet. Everyone watches the tower collapse as smoke billows. When the deceased has burned, a new procession forms to take the ashes to the sea.

Piodalan, a final cleansing of the soul, occurs several months later when more offerings are cast into the sea.

JAKARTA

0   1   2 kilometres
0   1 mile

Teluk Jakarta

Pelabuhan Sunda Kelapa

Taman Buaya Pluit

JALAN PROF. DR. TR SEDIYATMO

Soekarno Hatta

JALAN TELUK GONG

JALAN JEMBATAN

JALAN   LINGKAR   LUAR

JALAN GEDONG PANJANG

Pasar Ikan
Museum Bahari

Museum Wayang

JALAN LINGKAR LUAR

Taman Impian Jaya Ancol (Dunia Fantasi)
Jaya Ancol

JALAN LAKSAMANA

Taman Fatahillah
Museum Fatahillah
JALAN BANDENGAN
Museum Seni Rupa Jakarta
Stasiun Kota

JALAN MANGGA DUA RAYA

JALAN GUNUNG SAHARI

PANGERAN JAYAKARTA

Ciliwung

JAKARTA

JALAN PINTU BESAR

Glodok (Chinatown)

JALAN PROF. DR. LATUMENTEN

Gedung Arsip Nasional

JALAN GAJAHMADA

JALAN H. SAMANHUDI

Pasar Baru

JALAN PASAR BARU SELATAN

JALAN DAAN MOGOT

JALAN KYAITAPA

JALAN K. H. HASYIM ASYHARI

JALAN LET. JENDRAL S. PARMAN

Museum Puri Bhakti Renatama

JALAN VETERAN

Kathedral
Mesjid Istiqlal
Lapangan Banteng

JAKARTA

JALAN SURYOPRANOTO

Istana Merdeka & Istana Negara
MEDAN

JAKARTA PUSAT

Taman Anggrek Indonesia

JALAN TOMANG RAYA

Monumen Nasional (Monas)
Museum Pusat

MEDAN MERDEKA

Gereja Immanuel

JALAN PENING RAYA

Pasar Senen

JALAN PRAPATAN

JALAN TOL. JAKARTA MERAK

JALAN LET. JENDRAL S. PARMAN

Museum Tekstil

JALAN M. H. THAMRIN

JALAN H.O.S. COKROAMINOTO

JALAN IMAM BONJOL

Taman Ismail Marzuki

JALAN KRAMAT RAYA

JALAN DIPONEGORO

JALAN

Kios Barang Antik

JAKARTA BARAT

JALAN JENDRAL SUDIRMAN

JALAN JENDRAL GATOT SUBROTO

JALAN GERBANG PEMUDA

JALAN AFRIKA

Stadion Utama
Taman Anggrek Gelora Senayan

JALAN JENDRAL SUDIRMAN

JALAN H. RANGKAYO RASUNA SAID

JAKARTA SELATAN

JALAN DR. SAHARJO

JALAN PADE DA SUPOMO

JALAN ASIA

JALAN SISINGAMANGARAJA

Museum Abri Satria Mandala

JALAN SENOPATI

JALAN SURYO

JALAN JENDRAL GATOT SUBROTO

JALAN PANGLIMA POLIM RAYA

JALAN TRUNOJOYO

JALAN WIJAYA

JALAN KAPTEN. TENDEAN

JALAN BUKIT RAYA

JALAN LET.

Blok M

Kebun Binatang Ragunan

JAKARTA

A Rewarding Stop-over

Muslim Jakarta, the big, sprawling capital of Indonesia, is a different world from rural Bali. However, it is a fascinating place to stop off *en route* to Bali to experience another aspect of the varied land that is Indonesia.

Introduction

Jakarta has an unsalubrious reputation which deters tourism. There is no denying that it is hot (with 95 per cent humidity November–April), crowded (more than 9 million inhabitants), polluted (you grow old waiting in the traffic-jams) and parts of it stink.

On the plus side, Jakarta has excellent cheap food and a nightlife second to none. It abounds in marvellous, musty old museums and there are streets of antiques and handicrafts from all over the archipelago. Utara (north) Jakarta in particular has many curiosities from Old Batavia, (as Jakarta used to be called), and the harbour, filled with tall-masted *Bugis* schooners, has little changed in 500 years.

This is the tourist face of Jakarta. Downtown is a busy, modern business area of de luxe hotels, department stores and an estimated 400 banks. Covering 410 square miles (650 sq km), the city is roughly divided into: Utara Jakarta – Pelabuhan Sunda Kelapa (harbour) area and Old Batavia/Chinatown; Selatan (south) Jakarta – satellite city, higher income area: Timur (east) Jakarta – housing estates: and Barat (west) Jakarta – largely a trade and consumer

goods district.
Known as the 'Mother City' – *Ibn Kota* – Jakarta is the centre of government, commerce and industry. It is also the film, fashion and literacy centre – all the papers are printed here – and although Bali claims more tourists, it remains the main gateway to Indonesia.

History
Jakarta began life as a small trading port at the mouth of the Ciliwung river, today the **Kali Besar** area. In 1527 it was named 'Jayakarta' (Glorious Victory) by Fatahillah, a conquering Muslim prince who ousted the Hindu rajas (local Hindu inscriptions date from AD5).
In the early 1600s, a Dutch East India fleet established a trading post in 'Jayakarta'. Renaming it 'Batavia' (after a German tribe who once occupied the Dutch lowlands), they built a new town. Almost like a 'tropical Amsterdam', it had intersecting canals, a market square, *stadhuis* (town hall) and houses with red-tiled roofs.
Administrative buildings were constructed around a huge, grassy *padang*, now Medan Merdeka, or Merdeka Square. But because of its terrible climate, it was unsuitable for Europeans: more Dutch are said to have died there than in any other colony in Asia.
Much of Jakarta's post-1700s architecture has survived. Fatahillah Square (Taman Fatahillah), in particular, is a fascinating window on Old Batavia. Unfortunately, just as many elegant old Chinese residences have been demolished to make way for city planning. The plethora of city monuments – to the army, athletes and heroes – was built during the Soekarno era. Development has continued under President Suharto. The city's layout is hard to sort out, but once you know your way about in relation to Jalan MH Thamrin, the long, traffic-congested, central artery, Jakarta is relatively well planned. Construction continues unabated; some of the most important buildings (Grand Hyatt, Kartika Plaza, Sahid Jaya hotels, etc) are owned by the Suharto family. The word 'Jaya' after many names means 'success' in *Bahasa Indonesia* (the national language). Warts and all, Jakarta is a success story and the absence of hasslers is a big advantage when shopping and sightseeing (but watch out for pickpockets!).

Sightseeing
Jakarta is full of interesting old treasures, but because sights are scattered over the city, you need time and patience. Certain parts can be seen on foot, or by taxi, but you are urged to take a City Tour. A guide who knows his way about greatly simplifies sightseeing. Comprehensive coach tours lasting five to six hours are operated daily by Setia Tours and Travel, with hotel pick-up. Apexindo Express Tours and Travel Services arrange tailor-made visits of Jakarta and elsewhere. Or consult your hotel travel agency.
Apexindo Express, Office 49-

50-51, 3rd floor, east wing arcade, Borobodur Inter-Continental Hotel (tel: 376598-376524).
Setia Tours and Travel (Grayline), Jalan Pinangsia Raya, Glodok Plaza Block B No 1 (tel: 6390008-6492892).

WHAT TO SEE

GLODOK
area of Jalan Pintu Besar
This is the heart of 'old Chinatown' with Chinese temples and houses in back streets off the busy commercial centre. The temple complex known as the 'Temple of Golden Virtue', dating from the mid-17th century, is the focal point of the Chinese community. Explore on foot, daytime only. A good shopping and eating area.

ISTIQLAL MOSQUE
Medan Merdeka
Planted opposite the cathedral and overlooked by the Borobodur Inter-Continental hotel, this is Southeast Asia's biggest mosque, built by President Soekarno. English-speaking conducted tours are recommended if you have never been inside a mosque. Women must cover their heads with a scarf and all must discard shoes outside. Photography is permitted. *Closed*: Friday morning.

MEDAN MERDEKA
'Freedom Square' is one of the largest public squares in the world. In the centre, the lofty

Jakarta, where most of the people are Muslim, has the biggest mosque in Southeast Asia

National Monument occupies the geographical heart of Jakarta. Once a military parade ground, the huge park has been surrounded by state bureaucratic headquarters since Dutch times. To the north are the **Istana Negara** (State Palace) and **Istana Merdeka** (Freedom Palace). The modern parliament building is also on the square as is the National Museum.

◆◆
MONUMEN NASIONAL (NATIONAL MONUMENT)
Medan Merdeka
Known as MONAS, the marble

The soaring National Monument: the symbol of Indonesian independence

obelisk is 450 feet (137m) high, topped with a flame and coated in 35 kilos of gold. It symbolises Indonesia's independence struggle against the Dutch. Take the lift up (entrance charge) for a great view, and go early, before the coachloads of Japanese tourists arrive. There is a small museum beneath the monument, presenting Indonesia's history through a series of dioramas. In the Independence Hall, you can listen to the voice of Soekarno broadcasting the Declaration of Independence.
Open: daily 08.00–17.00 hrs. WC available.

◆◆◆
PASAR IKAN ✓

harbour area
Traffic is so bad around Taman Fatahillah, the main square of old Dutch Batavia, that it can be quicker to walk to **Pelabuhan Sunda Kelapa**, popularly known as **Pasar Ikan**, or fish market at the mouth of the Ciliwung river. It was formerly the harbour town of Sunda Kelapa where the Portuguese used to trade with the Hindu kingdom of Pajajaran in the 16th century. Until recently the fish catch was auctioned here in the early morning. It has now moved. Streets around the old auction hall are lined with shops selling nautical bric-a-brac, shells, coral and unfortunate dehydrated turtles. Walk down past the Museum Bahari (on your left) towards the harbour. An important inter-island port, the quay is lined with *Bugis*

Orchids create a blaze of colour in the Taman Anggrek Jakarta

schooners, a sight from another world. If you ask courteously, most sailors do not mind you coming on board to look around. Up to 100 feet (30m) long, the great sailing vessels are made in Kalimantan and South Sulawesi. Hawkers sell miniature boats and other marine artefacts. Now a putrid canal, the Ciliwung river opening into the bay was a vital means of transport inland in the 15th century. Other vestiges of Dutch dominion in Indonesia are shipyards and a 17th-century watch tower, **Gedung Syahbandar** (Harbourmaster's Office). For a small fee you can climb to the top of the tower and have a fine view of the port area. You look down on to two 16th-century warehouses forming the **Museum Bahari** (see **Museums** page 22). Wear old shoes to visit the harbour area. Avoid midday. There is a small charge for entry to the wharf area, payable at the toll-gate.

◆◆
TAMAN ANGGREK GELORA SENAYAN (ORCHID GARDEN)

Indonesia is well known for orchids and Taman Anggrek, situated in the Senayan Sports Complex, is a commercial orchid park open to the public. There are 100 species and orchid auctions are held at 02.00–03.00 hrs.
Open: daily from 09.00 hrs. Admission charge.
Other orchid parks are at Jalan Parman-Slipi and **Taman Mini Indonesia** (see **Excursions** page 24).

◆◆◆
TAMAN FATAHILLAH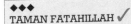

Old Batavia (or Kota)
This large, paved square overlooked by Jakarta City Museum (the former *stadhuis*)

was the main square in Dutch Batavia. Markets were held here and criminals punished, and early residents used to fetch water from the central well. Note the 16th-century Portuguese cannon (popularly called *Si Jagur* – 'Mr Sturdy') on the north side of the square. Its clenched fist symbol was believed to cure infertility – barren women used to sit astride the cannon and offer it flowers. The present cannon was recast from an earlier one. Today a busy 'flea market' is held around it.

Take your time in the vicinity of Fatahillah Square as there is much to see and enjoy, including the **Museum Fatahillah, Museum Seni Rupa** and **Museum Wayang** (City, Fine Arts and Puppet Museums – see **Museums** pages 23–24).

Artists at work in the local leisure spot Taman Impian Jaya Ancol

TAMAN IMPIAN JAYA ANCOL (ANCOL DREAMLAND)

There is a huge, open-air recreational park and crafts centre on Jakarta Bay. Basically for local families, it has the Disney-inspired **Dunia Fantasi**, including a swimming-pool, water-slides, oceanarium with performing dolphins, sealions and penguins, bowling complex, *warung* (food-stalls) and drive-in-theatre. There is also cottage accommodation and an 18-hole golf course. Excellent for children, but crowded at weekends. *Open:* daily. Admission charge.

Museums

Jakarta has many fascinating museums. The usual opening hours are Tuesday to Thursday

08.00–14.00 hrs; Friday to 11.00 hrs; Saturday to 13.00 hrs; Sunday to 15.00 hrs. Closed Monday. Entry charge, with extra for a camera.

These opening times are for guidance only, visitors should check locally before planning a trip to avoid disappointment.

MUSEUM BAHARI

near Pelabuhan Sunda Kelapa

This Marine Museum is in two restored 16th-century warehouses used by the Dutch East India Company to store tea, coffee, cloth, spices and other valuable exports from Java. One building exhibits trade memorabilia, the other deals with maritime history. There are some good model boats.

◆◆◆
MUSEUM FATAHILLAH
(CITY MUSEUM)
Taman Fatahillah
Built in 1627, the museum was formerly the *stadhuis*, or town hall, in Old Batavia. Rather dark and musty, the two-storey building oozes history – and suffering. Basements in the wings were the infamous 'water prisons' where prisoners were incarcerated in flooded cells. Note the window bars outside along Jalan Pintu Besar. Exhibits in the museum include Oriental and Dutch porcelain, coins, weapons and antique furniture. There are also portraits of former governor-generals, native princes and national heroes, plus displays of ancient maps.
Open: as given on page 22. For information tel: 67901.

◆◆◆
MUSEUM PUSAT
(NATIONAL MUSEUM) ✓

Jalan Merdeka Barat 12, Medan Merdeka
Built in the 18th century by the Batavian Society for Arts and Sciences, it houses the world's biggest exhibition of 'Indonesiana', with a huge collection of Oriental ceramics, models of traditional buildings and *prahu* (native sailing ships). See also the huge ethnic map representing many of Indonesia's different tribes, showing that in prehistoric times, Indonesia was connected by a land bridge to the Asian mainland. Bronzes are on the second floor, the Gold Room is only open on Sunday: highlights are the *kris* (daggers), handles studded with precious stones. *Open:* see page 22, except opens 08.30 hrs Tuesday to Thursday. For information tel: 360976.

◆◆
MUSEUM SENI RUPA JAKARTA
(FINE ARTS)
Jalan Taman Fatahillah 2
Housed in the old courts of justice, built in classic 19th-century Dutch colonial architectural style, the museum contains numerous art collections by Indonesia's finest painters, from the Raden Saleh era to contemporary times. There is also a ceramics museum (**Museum Keramik**). Descriptions are mainly in Indonesian. See in conjunction with the City and Puppet Museums.
All open: daily 08.00–14.00 hrs. (For information tel: 676090).

◆◆
MUSEUM TEKSTIL
(TEXTILE MUSEUM)
Jalan Satsuit Tuban 4
A display of handwoven textiles
from all over Indonesia is
housed in an ornate, 19th-
century house. A visit is
essential if you want to buy
fabrics. Every *batik* centre is
represented with an entire
room devoted to *ikat* (double-
weaving). There are also rare
textiles from remote islands in
the archipelago. The museum is
located in southwest Jakarta.
Open: Tuesday to Sunday
09.00–14.00 hrs. For information
tel: 365367.

◆
MUSEUM WAYANG
(PUPPET MUSEUM)
Jalan Pintu Besar Utara 27
Housed in a former church, the
museum exhibits *wayang*
(shadow puppets) and dolls –
both highly developed art-
forms in Indonesia. There is also
puppetry from other Asian
countries. Performances take
place in the rear of the museum
every alternate Sunday
morning. Photography is
permitted at a charge.
Open: usual times (see page 22)
except closes 14.00 hrs Sunday.
For information tel: 679560.

Other 'special interest' museums
are: **Museum Perangko**
(stamps); **Museum Abri Satria
Mandala** (armed forces), Jalan
Gatot Subroto (opposite the
Kartika Chandra Hotel); **Gedung
Arsip Nasional Museum**,
(national archives), Jalan
Gajahmada 111; **Museum Puri
Bhrakti Renatama** (Presidential,
with a collection of state gifts).

Churches
Driving about Jakarta, you will
pass several interesting old
churches, including:
St Mary's Kathedral, Jalan
Kathedral 7. On the north side of
Benteng Square facing the
newer Istiqlal Mosque, it is 19th-
century, restored (Catholic).
Gereja Immanuel, Jalan
Merdeka Timur 10, east side of
Merdeka Square. Dutch
Protestant built in the 1830s, it
has an English service, Sunday
17.00 hrs.
Sion Church: Jalan Pangeran
Jayakarta 1, near Fatahillah
Square. Built in the late 17th
century for the Portuguese
community in Old Batavia.
Known as the 'Portuguese
Church', it is Jakarta's oldest.
View the interior Tuesday to
Saturday, 09.00–15.00 hrs.

Excursions

◆◆◆
TAMAN MINI INDONESIA
(BEAUTIFUL INDONESIA
IN MINIATURE)

*7½ miles (12km) south of city
centre*
Indonesia's answer to
Disneyland is the most popular
trip to make from Jakarta. A
huge open-air cultural and
amusement park, it covers 295
acres (120 hectares). From the
city it is a 30-to 60-minute drive,
depending on the traffic.
Pavilions built in traditional
styles act as a window on the
customs and lifestyles of
Indonesia's 27 provinces. The
complex features a museum,
theatre, bird park, orchid
garden, miniature train rides,

open-sided trams, cable cars and boating. It surrounds a man-made lake, landscaped to represent the archipelago. Obtain a programme to see what's on; there are special Cultural Shows on Sunday. Near the entrance is the **Indonesia Museum** built in traditional Balinese-style architecture. It is the best displayed museum in Indonesia. On the ground floor is a spectacular exhibition of national dress and wedding costumes from every region. Other displays include a Balinese tooth-filing ceremony and hunting implements from Timor (1st floor) and traditional weaving tools, superb *ikat* textiles and silverware from east Java and Bali (3rd floor). Look up at the superbly carved roof depicting a lotus flower: central Javanese craftwork. Do not miss the sculpture of a man and his fighting cock carved from a single piece of *johar* wood which took Igusti Mede Bawa, Indonesia's most famous wood-carver two years to sculpt. No Photography.

Within Taman Mini is a huge **Bird Park** with over 500 native species and one Spanish flamingo in spacious walk-through aviaries. Do not miss the birds of paradise, hornbills, and crested pigeons. The stream represents the Wallace line, symbolically dividing the birds inhabiting eastern and western zones.

Clean WCs available.

Taman Mini is clean and well laid-out. You will need a day to see it thoroughly. Miss the shops, but eat at the *warung* (food-stalls). Avoid at weekends.

Open: 09.00–16.00 hrs daily. Entry charge with extra fees for cable car rides, tours by ox-cart and the swimming pool.

Crested pigeons, with their luminous blue plumage, are among Taman Mini's beautiful birds

Several tour operators include Taman Mini in a daily tour. Independent travellers take bus 408 from outside Sarinah Department Store, Jalan MH Thamrin, to Cilitan Terminal. Then catch red mini-bus no 2, marked TMII. Allow one hour. Do not consider Taman Mini is only for children; it is highly recommended to adults.

Other excursions, for shorter or longer stays are:

KEBUN BINATANG RAGUNAN (RAGUNAN ZOO)

Jalan Ragunan, Pasar Minggu area

About nine miles (15km) from the city, this small, but interesting collection, kept in habitat enclosures rather than cages, includes Komodo dragons, dwarf buffalo, pygmy monkeys and orang-utans. There are also native birds and lizards. The botanical garden is worth a visit.

Open: daily 08.00–18.00 hrs. Avoid weekends. Amenities include food-stalls, shade and WCs.

LUBANG BUAYA

10 miles (16km) southeast of Jakarta

Tours visit this massive monument *en route* to Taman Mini Indonesia. It commemorates the murder of six Indonesian generals killed in the abortive Communist coup of 1 October 1965. Their mutilated corpses were stuffed down the well, or *lubang*. Thought-provoking. Entry charge.

◆◆◆
PULAU SERIBU (THOUSAND ISLANDS) ✓

Pulau Seribu comprises 118 tropical islands dotted across the vast expanse of Jakarta Bay. It has better beaches than Bali, but the islands suffer from a lack of publicity. Day-trips are available, but when you reach the islands – Seba, Putri or Pelangi – you will wish to spend the night ... and the next ... The only let-down is the poor cooking, but catch your own fish and they will cook it. Only seven of the islands are inhabited, by fishermen whose nets you pass on the boat trip. All are ringed by coral with good skin-diving off the beach, or scuba-diving from a wooden *prahu*. The entire area is a National Marine Park and home to many birds and also *biawaks*, a smaller cousin (one metre long) of the Komodo dragon.

The climate is tropical with average temperature 32°C (90°F). Best months are April to September – August is crowded. Casual beachwear is worn day and evenings. A dive-shop hires out equipment and you can buy a diving package with an Indonesian companion. Take gear if you plan to fish. *Three islands are packaged by Biltour Cruise Division, ground floor lobby, Hyatt Aryaduta, Jalan Prapatan, Jakarta.*

Pelangi. 32 acres (13 hectares), 50 miles (80km) from Jakarta. White sand beach, tropical growth, 29 large, comfortable, air-conditioned cottages with hot shower, 220V electricity, radio. Meals in attractive

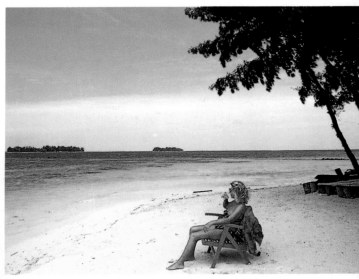

Pulau Seribu (Thousand Islands) – a desert island fantasy come true

restaurant and a natural aquarium in the reef. Licensed. Visited by overseas cruise ships. Moderately expensive.
Putri. Ten minutes by *prahu* from Pelangi. 17 acres (7 hectares) with 31 air-conditioned cottages in lovely surroundings. Fishing and diving available. A resident doctor is shared with Pelangi and Seba. Moderately expensive.
Seba. Lying opposite Putri. Ten acres (4 hectares) and, like the other islands, traffic-free. There are no shops or police. 25 basic, clean, comfortable bungalows under palms and she-oaks. The bar-restaurant with 'muzak' and TV needs a good chef. Ideal for nature-lovers with a natural island aquarium containing fish and small sharks; turtle-breeding programme; birds and *biawaks*. Moderate.

There are daily departures from Ancol Dreamland marina by speedboat. Ferries take nearly four hours. Daily charter flights from Halim airport to Pulau Panjang take 25 minutes. From here there is a ferry on to Pulau Putri.

PRACTICALITIES

Accommodation

The location of your hotel is the key to sightseeing in Jakarta. It is also advisable to pay more than usual for safe, comfortable accommodation. Cheaper establishments are often noisy and dirty. Backpacker-type *losmen* (rooms to let) along Jalan Jaksa attract various undesirables.

JAKARTA

Luxury Class
Borobodur Inter-Continental,
Jalan Lapangan Banteng Selatan,
Jakarta 10710 (tel: 3805555).
Large hotel with attractive
décor, huge lobby with shops
and Apexindo Travel Agency.
Near the central Mosque and 15
minutes by taxi from the
commercial area.
Jakarta Hilton, Jalan Jendral
Gatot Subroto, Senayan, Jakarta
10002 (tel: 583051). Tastefully
decorated rooms overlook lush
tropical gardens. Located 15
minutes by taxi to central
Jakarta and includes
restaurants, shopping plaza,
large swimming pool, nine

*Poolside luxury is provided at the
Hyatt Aryaduta in Jakarta*

tennis courts and three squash
courts. Highly recommended to
business travellers. There is
a 'Lady Hilton' check-in and
private floor for women
guests.
Hyatt Aryaduta, Jalan Prapatan
44–48, Jakarta 10110 (tel:
376008). Hotel with 340 rooms
in one of the best locations in
Jakarta, only 35 minutes from
the airport, 10 minutes by taxi to
the banking district, and within
walking distance of the good
shopping area, National
Monument and museums. Rear
rooms have a view of the river.
Regency VIP service available.
Good choice of restaurants.
Excellent security. Business
centre.
Grand Hyatt Jakarta, Jalan
Thamrin Kav 28–30, Jakarta
10230 (tel: 3107400). Exclusive
hotel in central business district.
450 grand rooms including 18
executive suites. Jakarta's
leading rendezvous –
O'Reiley's Bar and Pub highly
recommended. Seafood,
Japanese and Han Cantonese
restaurants. Tropical gardens
surround a huge pool,
gymnasium, roof-garden
jogging track, 6 tennis courts.
Conference facilities for 800
guests.
Airport: 45 minutes by car.
Limousine service.
Citraland, Jalan S. Parman,
Jakarta 11470 (tel: 5660640).
335 rooms, TV/video, coffee/tea
making facilities. Located near
the airport and Jakarta's
industrial area – recommended
for business and in-transit
travellers. Well-run Swiss
management. Access to multi-
storey shopping mall.

First Class
Hotel Indonesia, Jalan MH Thamrin, Jakarta 10310 (tel: 3906262). Good-value government-owned hotel. Just 10 minutes' walk to Sarinah Department Store and five minutes by taxis to the commercial area, banks, offices, etc.
President, Jalan MH Thamrin 59, Jakarta 10350 (tel: 320508). Owned by JAL (Japanese Airlines), it receives mainly Japanese guests. Good location.
Sari Pacific, Jalan MH Thamrin, Jakarta (tel: 323707). Also on Jakarta's main road near banks and shops. Average rooms.

Tourist Class
Hotel Menteng I, Jalan Gondangdia Lama 28 (tel: 325208). Has 150 pleasant rooms; check first as some are airless. Small pool, friendly atmosphere.
Hotel Menteng II, Jalan Cikini Raya 105 (tel: 325540). Pleasant for what it offers. In a busy area and with a tiny pool. Poor foreign exchange rate at both Menteng hotels.
Marco Polo, Jalan Cik Ditiro (tel: 325409). Near Jalan Surabaya 'antiques street' and with 181 reasonable rooms. Popular with Japanese groups. Overseas calls must be paid for in cash. Good value.
Putri Duyung Cottages, Taman Impian Jaya Ancol (tel: 680108). Individual cottages on Jakarta Bay, popular with executives using Ancol golf course. Also excellent for families – kitchens, video programmes, water-slides and oceanarium in Ancol. Central Jakarta is 30-50 minutes

by taxi. Good value, but isolated for an independent traveller.
Sabang Metropolitan Hotel, Jalan Agus Salim (tel: 3857621). Pleasant, medium-sized hotel. Excellent location near shops and restaurants.
Wisata International, Jalan MH Thamrin (tel: 320308). In the city centre near Grand Hyatt. Good value, but no atmosphere.

Economy
Hotel Pasarbaru, Jalan Pasar Baru Selatan 6 (tel: 366474). Small, clean, modern hotel in busy Pasar Baru (night market area). Recommended to budget travellers. Ask for rear room.
Karya Hotel, Jalan Jaksa 32–34 (tel: 320484). The most expensive in a range of backpacker-type *losmen* on Jalan Jaksa – 15 minutes' walk to the city centre. Cheap enough, but not clean enough.
Transaera Hotel, Jalan Merdeka Timur 16 (tel: 351373). Old-style hotel set back on a busy road. Near shops and National Monument. Comfortable, though drab rooms. Indonesian food only.
Wisma Ise, Jalan Wahid Hasyim 168 (tel: 333463). 20 quiet rooms located off Jalan MH Thamrin, Jakarta's main thoroughfare.

Nightlife and Entertainment
Jakarta's nightlife is second to none in South-East Asia. It ranges from select cocktail lounges, to lively karaoke bars, discos and a Las Vegas-style floorshow staged at the Hailai Executive Club, Jalan Lodan, near Ancol Dreamland (tel: 689868). The biggest

concentration of nightspots is in Chinatown.

Popular lounges are: The Clipper Lounge (Mandarin Oriental Hotel), Sting Music Lounge (Jayakarta Tower Hotel), Garden Lounge (Jakarta Hilton), Ambassador Lounge (Hyatt Aryaduta), Ganesha Bar (Hotel Indonesia), Pendopo Lounge (Borobudur ICH) and Ria Lounge (Sahid Jaya Hotel).

Pub Crawls

Most bars open from noon until around 02.00 hours. 'Happy hours' offer discounted drinks between 17.00 and 20.00 hours. Drinking holes range from rough to élite. Measures are generous. All bars have a décor theme with live entertainment likely to be Filipino. Also suggested: **After 8**, **Jaya Pub**, **Amigos**, **Rumours**, **Topaz**. **O'Reiley's Pub** in the Grand Hyatt is the 'in-place' in Jakarta. A huge number of massage bars/discos are found on Jalan Mangga Besar in Chinatown; they include **Valentino**, **Fairy Garden**, **Our Place**, etc. *Karaoke* bars are the rage: **OK! Karaoke 2** is recommended (18.00–04.00 hours).

Discos

Jakarta boasts some of the biggest discos in Asia. The **Regent Space Palace** holds 4,000. Currently popular are: **Oriental Disco**, **Voila**, **Fire**, **Tanamur Disco**, **Le Mirage**, **Ebony**, **My Place**, **Rumours** and the **Stardust Disco** in the Jayakarta Tower Hotel. Cover normally includes beer, or a soft drink.

Night-clubs/Cabaret

Nirwana Supper Club (Hotel Indonesia), Dinner, western cabaret, city views.
Blue Ocean Restaurant and Nite Club, Jalan Hayam Wuruk 5. Bright, crowded, choice of 300 hostesses.
Blue Moon, Jalan Gajah Madah.
LCC Nite Club, opposite the National Monument.
Sky Room, Duta Merlin Shopping Centre, Chinatown.

Evening Tours

There is a choice of several tours. **Jakarta After Dark** (minimum of two persons) is operated by Panorama nightly. Four hours' duration. Includes dinner, cultural performance and disco. **Grayline Night-Club** tour includes oriental cabaret and night-club. Five hours' duration; tour fare includes dinner and a drink.

Indonesian Cultural Performances

For *Wayang Orang* and *Ketoprak* (Javanese dance dramas) performances visit Bhatara Theatre at Jalan Kalilio. *Wayang Orang* is staged nightly from 20.15 to midnight except on Monday and Thursday nights.

Wayang Kulit (shadow puppet plays) and *Wayang Golek* (three-dimensional puppet shows) are staged alternately at the National Museum, Jalan Merdeka Barat on Sunday evenings starting at 20.00 hours. At the Wayang Museum the play begins at 10.00 hrs on Sunday mornings.

The *Srimulat Show* is a popular Javanese comedy show, staged nightly from 20.00–23.00 hrs at Taman Ria Senayan.

The *Miss Tjitjih Show* is a

West. The largest, attached to the Citraland Hotel, is called the **Citraland Mall**. **Matahari** is the biggest department store within the complex which as well as 300 shops contains a health centre, nightclub, cinema and a variety of restaurants. The **Plaza Indonesia** is a modern complex including the Sogo department store. It is attached to the Grand Hyatt Hotel in central Jakarta. **Pondok Indah Mall** is another large, up-market shopping complex housing the Metro Department Store, Marks and Spencers and cafés, restaurants and cinemas. The new **Blok M Mall** with the Pasaraya (big and beautiful) Department Store is rising in prominence. Street stalls here sell local bargains and smart shops offer designer goods – note many brand names are fakes. Another favourite is the multi-storey **Sarinah Department Store** chain on Jalan Thamrin and Jalan Iskandarsyah II 2, Kemayoran Baru, Jakarta.

Gajahmada Plaza, Jalan Gajahada, is another exclusive shopping complex for imports, jewellery, etc, 10-30 minutes by taxi from central Jakarta. Also in Chinatown, the **Duta Merlin Shopping Centre**, Jalan Gajahmada is recommended. Other good shopping centres are: **Ratu Plaza**, **Ramayana Department Store** (at several locations in the city). A cheap, interesting shopping complex is **Pasar Rama**. Curious visitors may be interested in a vast, wholesale cake auction, held daily there at 03.00–05.00 hrs. You have to be keen. Good general buys (later) are clothes, trainers or gym boots, fruit and

Jakarta's markets are lively and interesting, and add to the variety and colour of the city

vegetables. Any taxi driver will know the locations.

Adresses of other shopping areas and centres are:

Aldiron Plaza, Jalan Melawai, Kemayoran Baru.

Hayam Wuruk Plaza, Jalan Hayam Wuruk.

Pasar Senen, located at Jalan Pasar Senen, provides all kinds of textiles, electric fixtures, ready made dresses, etc.

Pasar Tanah Abang, not far from Sarinah Department Store. This shopping centre provides all kinds of textiles and *batiks*.

Bookshops/Stationery/Newspapers

All tourist hotels have a bookshop selling books about Indonesia, magazines, postcards etc. Prices are often 15-20 per cent more than in outside shops. Near the Hyatt Aryaduta is the **Gunung Agung**, Jakarta's oldest and biggest bookshop and stationers. Better hotels deliver local English-language papers to your room. **Gramedia**, Jalan Gajahmada (Chinatown) and Jalan Melawai (Blok M) has the best English-language selection, but do not depend on finding something of interest. Kwitang district is Jakarta's bookshop area.

Clothes Markets

A lively clothes market is held around the Portuguese cannon on Taman Fatahillah, daily except Sunday, 06.00–15.00 hrs. Also **Manga Dua** Market in Chinatown and Pasar Baru which sells everything as well as fabrics, 'Polo' sportswear, Kelvin Klein copies, and the inevitable Lacoste designs. Indonesia makes excellent, bargain-priced gym-boots. Try **Pasar Rama** – at Senen (Monday).

Cassettes and Photographic

Excellent recordings of Western classical, jazz, rock, and pop music, plus Indonesian selections are available at half European prices. There are good shops in Blok M (especially in the Aldiron Plaza) and Jalan Agus Salim. The latter street also has many photographic shops selling all types of film. Even professional film can be bought at **Jakarta Foto**, No 35A. English spoken. Good, cheap, fast developing of prints.

Sport

During your stay in Jakarta you need not miss your favourite sports. There are a number of sport centres and golf courses, and bowling is particularly popular here.

Golf Courses

Jakarta Golf Club, Jalan Rawamangun Muka Raya (tel: 4891208 or 4895298).
Padang Golf Jaya Ancol, Jalan Lodan Timur Ancol (tel: 681121).
Halim Golf Course, Lanuma Halim Perdanakusuma (tel: 800729, 800793).
Kemayoran Golf Course, Jalan Asia Afrika Senayan (tel: 582508, 581695).
Pondok Indah Golf and Country Club, Jalan Metro Pondok Indah, Kemayoran Lama (tel: 764906, 762802, 766962).
Jagorawi Golf and Country Club (tel: 581001).
Sawangan Country Club, Jalan Raya Sawangan – Parung (tel: 742193).

Squash

Courts are available at: Borobodur Inter-Continental Hotel, Jakarta Hilton Hotel, Mandarin Oriental Hotel and the Grand Hyatt Jakarta Hotel.

Bowling

Jaya Ancol Bowling Centre. Kartika Chandra Bowling Centre. Monas Bowling Centre and Kemayoran Baru Bowling Centre.

Swimming

Available at international standard hotels; Jaya Ancol Dreamland; Senayan Swimming Pool; Kelapa Gading Sport Centre; Grogol Sport Centre; Kuningan Sport Centre; Taman Mini Indonesia Indah.

WHAT TO SEE ON BALI

Bali has many faces, and the visitor may wish to glimpse all of these or perhaps get to know just one or two. There is certainly something for all interests and the gazetteer that follows gives plenty of detail. But first, a brief description of what Bali has to offer may be helpful in the planning of itineraries.

In the south, the capital **Denpasar** is the main business and administrative centre, and the **Kuta-Legian** and **Sanur-Semawang** areas are popular beach resorts. Watersports, shopping and nightlife are the highlights.

The **Nusa Dua Bukit Peninsula** is an emerald earring off south Bali. It includes an international tourist complex, a port and a rugged coastline. Watersports are enjoyed here, especially surfing off **Ulu Watu**.

Central Bali is the cultural heartland of the island, centred on **Ubud-Mas** and local villages. Here the pleasures are arts and crafts, shopping, lush scenery and beautiful rural walks.

The **East Coast** has picturesque beach resorts with good watersports, especially diving. There are also relics of ancient kingdoms and fine views.

The **West Coast** sees few visitors. Plantation farming is carried out in jungle clearings. The surfing beaches are undeveloped.

The **North Coast** is a drier region with black sand beaches and good diving. This, the area of the old Dutch capital, remains uncommercialised.

The **Central Mountain region** is cool, moist and green with quiet lakes, gently smoking volcanoes and important temples. It is an area for trekking.

Nusa Penida and **Nusa Lembongan** islands off southeast Bali enjoy a rustic lifestyle. Quiet coral islands, they have good surfing.

Notes

Sites such as temples or caves are always accessible to visitors. During normal visiting times (roughly 08.00–18.00 hrs), there may be a custodian on duty to whom you will be expected to pay an entrance fee or donation.

The words *bemo* and *losmen*, which occur throughout the gazetteer, may be unfamiliar. For explanations see pages 121 and 93.

West and Far East come together in the architecture of Agung Karangasem in Amlapura

WHAT TO SEE ON BALI

◆◆
AMLAPURA
East Coast

Amlapura lies inland, 10 minutes from the sea. It is a journey of about three and a half hours from Denpasar via Gianyar and Candi Dasa. Amlapura was known as Karangasem until the eruption of Gunung Agung in 1963. The superstitious Balinese changed its name in the hope of averting another eruption. The town is spread out, with a large, clean residential area and small, downhill business centre.

The Kingdom of Karangasem, which seceded from the Gelgel kingdom in the 17th century, became the most powerful kingdom in Bali. **Agung Karangasem** is an early 20th-century palace also known as Puri Kanginan. It was owned by the last rajas of Karangasem before the Dutch takeover.

Accommodation
Amlapura is not a place to stay. Travellers visit it from either Candi Dasa or Tirtagangga.

Food and Drink
Lenny's is a 'tourist-type' restaurant.

Travelling On
The bus-*bemo station* is at the end of the shopping district where the road descends to Ujung. Buses terminate at Amlapura, but there is a red *bemo*-service on to **Singaraja**. **Tirtagangga** is a 15 minutes' drive. The Amlapura-Rendang road is half a mile (1km) out of Amlapura. This is a quiet, less travelled route across to Besakih (the Mother Temple – see page 42) via the market town of **Bebandem**. The short diversion to **Putung** is worth making for the good views on a clear day.

BALINA BEACH see **CANDI DASA**

BANGLI
central-eastern Bali, 26 miles (42km) from Denpasar
The town is *en route* to Lake Batur, halfway up the slope to Penelokan (see page 63). Expect traffic congestion until you pass Gianyar. There is a good road surface to Penelokan, and rich farmland scenery. Today an unprepossessing town, in the 12th century Bangli was capital of a Balinese kingdom. It is worth visiting for **Pura Kehen**, a terraced temple, reached up a long flight of steps. The temple's walls are inlaid with the remains of bright pieces of chipped Chinese porcelain similar to temple decoration in Bangkok. The upper sanctuary has 11 tapering *merus*, resting places of the gods. A shrine houses thrones for the Hindu deities, Brahma, Shiva and Vishnu. There is a small museum.

Accommodation
Bangli is not an overnight stop but if you need a bed, try the **Artha Sastra** in the town centre, opposite the busy *bemo* station. A former royal residence, it is a pleasant traditional-style inn and is cheap.

Food and Drink
Try the **night market** (opposite the Artha Sastra).

Entertainment
There are occasional dance performances and exhibits for groups in the arts complex, down the road from Pura Kehen.

Side-Trips
Bukit Demulih. The hill of this name is one hour's walk along the road to Tampaksiring. There are great rice terraces and coastal panoramas to view from the top.
Pura Dalem. This temple of the dead with grotesque reliefs is 15 minutes' walk on the road to Gianyar.

Travelling On
There are frequent minibus and *bemo* services to surrounding places of interest, such as **Kintamani** 20 miles (33km), **Klungkung** 11½ miles (19km), **Besakih** 13 miles (21km). **Warning**: There have been incidents involving robbery and trickery in the Bangli district. Car-drivers and *bemo* passengers need to be alert.

BATUBULAN
central Bali, 6 miles (10km) from Denpasar
Here you will see stonemasons working in roadside factories. Many antique/second-hand shops line the busy Ubud-Gianyar road. **Oka**, **Antik Kembar** and **Indra Antiques** are suggestions, if you are interested in this kind of purchase.

BEDUGAL
Central Highlands
The village lies at 5,000 feet (1,500m) above sea-level, in Tabanan District and is about four hours' drive from Denpasar. Bedugal is on Lake Bratan which fills the crater of Gunung Bratan. Cool and peaceful, it is a perfect foil to the humid coast.

The mountain air of Bedugal village, on Lake Bratan, is refreshingly welcome

Uludanu Temple at Candi Kuning on Lake Bratan just over a mile (2km) north of Bedugal is half-Hindu, half-Buddhist. It is dedicated to Dewi Danu (Goddess of Water).

Bukit Mungsu is an orchid market below Bedugal. Livestock and fruit and vegetables are also sold there.

Kebun Raya, near the market, is a botanical garden and orchid collection.

Accommodation and Eating

Bukit Mungsu Indan. Set back from the lake on a hill, this is plain but comfortable. Rear cottages have a wonderful panorama overlooking Bedugal valley. Restaurant and bar. Moderate.

Hotel Bedugal. Picturesque lakeshore location, but spoilt by groups of noisy people. Moderately cheap. A restaurant overlooking the lake is pleasant at night. Eat here rather than the restaurant on the hill whose waiter has to trudge down (and up) with every order.

Lila Graha (tel: 25750). This lofty spot above the lake is potentially charming. It has a restaurant and bar. Moderately cheap.

Pancasari Inn (tel: 34875/33962). Thirty minutes' walk from the lake, it has 11 rooms.
Peaceful and comfortable with restaurant and bar; tennis, golf course near by. Suitable for couples rather than solitary travellers. Expensive.

Activities

You can walk around lakes Bratan, Tablingan and Buyan, about 16½ miles (27km). Swimming in the lakes is a chilly experience. If fishing is your scene, rod and worms can be bought locally. Boating trips by speedboat (minimum four persons) or motorised *prahu* can be made at a cost. Bali Handara Golf and Country Club has an 18-hole golf course surrounded by jungle.

Travelling On
There are *bemo* connections to Singaraja, Denpasar etc.

BENOA
Nusa Dua Bukit peninsula
Bali's small port lies on the tip of a shallow bay at the end of the airport runway, 20 minutes' drive south of Sanur. The Bali International Yacht Club will interest anyone wanting to crew: it boasts a notice board, clean WCs and a small licensed restaurant. There are *prahus* for rent to visit Serangan Island – expensive.

BESAKIH
central-northeastern Bali, 37 miles (60km) from Denpasar
The first mention of **Pura Besakih** is AD 1007. It has been the central Balinese 'Mother Temple' since the 15th-century Gelgel dynasty. The temple complex is 3,300 feet (1,000m) up Gunung Agung. Steep twin stairways ascend seven rising terraces containing about 30 different shrines. Visitors are forbidden to enter the inner courtyards. Besakih is disappointing, even melancholic on a dull, misty day.

Getting There
There is a frequent *bemo* service from Klungkung, and Besakih is also approached from Bangli, or Tirtagangga. Self-drivers take the left fork

(ignore the 'No Entry' sign), half a mile (1km) before the top. You will be charged for parking and on entry a donation will be requested.
It is a steep walk from the ticket-house up to the temple. Easy-riders charge a fee to pillion you to the base on motorcycles. Ride up and walk down. You have to run the gauntlet of souvenir sellers, whose shops line the path to the temple. The trip is tough for older travellers.

Accommodation
Three miles (5km) below Besakih is the simple **Arca Valley Inn**, which is a base for the climb up Gunung Agung (see below).

Food and Drink
The parking lot is ringed by clean cafés. Stalls sell bananas, *salak* and *mangosteen* (see page 89).

Climbing Gunung Agung
The volcano is over 10,000 feet (3,000m) high, and rises six miles (10km) behind Besakih. Fit climbers should manage the trip in 10 hours. Basic requirements are: a flashlight, weatherproof jacket, good walking boots, water and supplies such as sweets or fruits. Depart at 05.00 hours to get back before dusk and take a guide as lower trails are confusing in the dark. Much of the ascent is vertical; the middle section traverses humid jungle and the upper part is over lichen-covered rocks. The final ridge is narrow and there is room only for one person at a time to stand on the summit. But there is never a crowd. The peak is very cold and you

should take into account that rain may obscure the view. The volcano remains active – the last eruption was 16 May 1963. Alternatively, make it a two-day trip and stay overnight on the mountainside, at **Tirtha Mas**, where holy water is collected (ask your guide).

◆
BLAHBATUH
East Coast
Inland junction for Gianyar, Bona. The **Pura Gaduh** temple here is a reconstruction – the original was destroyed in an earthquake in 1917. It houses an ancient stone head, reputedly portraying Kebo Iwa, a legendary giant.

◆
BONA
central Bali
About 12½ miles (20km) from Denpasar, on a back road between Gianyar and Blahbatuh, the village itself is insignificant, but bamboo furniture is an important industry. Woven palm-leaf articles are another local product. You can see a *kechak* (see page 96) and other dances there – tickets and transport from Ubud.

◆
BUKIT JAMBA
central Bali
This is a scenic point, five miles (8km) north of Klungkung *en route* to Besakih on a quiet road. It has a garden restaurant and WC on the right, up steep steps. Stop at the lay-by opposite the restaurant for a view down the valley, to the sea.

Fishing and sailing are popular activities in Candi Dasa

◆◆◆
CANDI DASA ✓

East Coast
The journey takes about 1½-2 hours from Denpasar. Traffic is bad until Klungkung. There is coastal scenery from Kusamba. A quiet fishing village until recently, Candi Dasa now counts more than 50 *losmens*, restaurants and ancillaries to a tourist trade. It is not yet spoilt like Kuta, but this seems likely. The village of Candi Dasa stretches for a mile (2km) along the palm-fringed coast. A drawback is no beach. At high tide the sand disappears and you must sunbathe on rough sea walls. A small lagoon by the

Amlapura exit marks the end of town. There is a bank, post office and several souvenir shops.

Accommodation

Candi Dasa is a good alternative sightseeing base to Kuta, or Sanur, although it is more for younger travellers. Check that your room, the restaurant, or bar is not falling into the sea. Erosion is bad along the seafront.

Candi Dasa Beach Bungalows. Pleasant, but as with many hotels, the bungalows are too close together. Moderate to cheap.

Homestay Ida. Pleasant, airy cottages by the lagoon. Moderate.

Rama Lakeside Bungalows. On a picturesque lagoon site. The upstairs rooms are more private; ask for Room 1. Moderate to cheap.

Rama Ocean View Bungalows. Modern cottage complex catering to tour-groups. Moderate.

An option is to stay outside Candi Dasa at **Balina Beach**, two miles (3km) away, where there is excellent swimming, sailing and diving.

Nelayan Village Bungalows/Balina Diving Centre, Office: Jalan Raya Batujimbar 129, Sanur, Bali (telex: 35307). A variety of rooms from cheap to family-style suites. Pleasant and comfortable, with a restaurant and bar. The centre specialises in diving and guests are mainly

The Puri Buitan Hotel at Balina Beach, Denpasar is run with families in mind

divers. There are qualified Scuba instructors, and an advanced open-water dive course of four to five days is available. English, German, Dutch spoken. Advance booking required.

Puri Buitan Hotel, PO Box 444, Denpasar (tel: (361) 87182). A clean, modern hotel on the beach with 34 simple fan-cooled rooms. It is ideal for families. Tours arranged. Licensed restaurant. Swimming pool.

Food and Drink

Eating out in Candi Dasa restaurants is very much a hit and miss affair.

Ibu Rasmini Warung near the lagoon has a cheap, Indonesian-style menu with *nasi goreng* etc. Seafood is hard to find. **TJ's** is a more expensive restaurant in central Candi Dasa. Tables are on platforms set around fish-ponds. Eclectic menu and loud music.

Nightlife

There are several bars and two low-key discos. People generally go to bed early in Candi Dasa.

Activities

Scuba Diving is available off offshore islets; see also Balina Diving Centre above (under **Accommodation**).

Snorkelling fans can observe reef life in safe conditions about 100 yards/metres off shore. There is excellent **swimming** from Balina Beach, and for **sailing** enthusiasts *prahus* are available at Balina Beach, or from Candi Dasa lagoon. You can **walk** to Balina Beach (2 miles/3km) or, alternatively,

inland to Tenganan (4 miles/6km – see page 69).

Short road trips can be made to Amlapura, Tirtagangga and Besakih.

Shopping

The souvenir shops are harbingers of Kuta-style commerce (see page 57). There is *ikat*-weaving in Tenganan (see page 69).

CANGGU

Southwest Coast about 7½ miles (12km) from Denpasar

A lovely road-trip through the rice-fields ends on a black sand surfing beach – the reason for visiting Canggu. Stay on the main road: side-roads are terrible. A name without any apparent village, Canggu has one basic hotel:

Perenan Beach Hotel. Four rooms with shared bathroom/WC. Simple restaurant with drinks. This establishment is often full. An ideal place for backpackers or surfies.

CELUK

Central southeastern Bali about 40 minutes from Denpasar

Celuk is Bali's silver centre. Take your pick of dozens of workshops along the road. A quiet place to watch silversmiths is Cemengan Village. Most designs are traditional, but some are influenced by Western tastes. Coming from Denpasar, turn left at a roadsign 'Ana' and continue 110 yards (100m).

See the silversmiths, walk around the village and visit the temple.

◆
CULIK
Northeast Coast
This is a transit stop on the
Tirtagangga-Tulamben road.
There are rice-terraces and
views of Gunung Agung (see
page 42). Beyond Culik, the old
lava flow from the volcano
descends right down to the sea.
For anyone feeling the need for
a quick dip, there is a beach
near Culik village.

◆◆
DENPASAR
southern Bali
The capital and main town,
(population around 300,000),
Denpasar used to be a
charming old tree-lined town,
where people commuted by
dokar, or donkey-cart. The
name *den pasar* means 'beside
the market'. Dusty, noisy and
polluted by traffic fumes, it is
now a place travellers avoid.

Allow Denpasar one day: it has some fine museums.

Sightseeing

Bali Museum

Jalan May Wisnu, off Puputan Square

Founded by the Dutch in 1932, separate pavilions feature traditional temple and palace architecture. In the second courtyard, is a large building in the style of an old royal pavilion of the Karangasem kingdom. Styles from Singaraja and Tabanan are also represented. Exhibits range from Balinese stone-age artefacts to modern works. Special features are stone sculptures, dance masks and scale models of ceremonial events. Towering Barong Landung figures are represented (see page 96). *Open*: Tuesday, Wednesday, Thursday, Sunday 08.00–14.00 hrs; and Friday 08.00–11.00 hrs; Saturday 08.00–12.30 hrs. Closed Monday.

Taman Budaya (Art Centre)

Easily found on Jalan Nusa Indah in east Denpasar, its galleries include a permanent exhibition of Balinese painting. The centre is set in picturesque grounds and the complex includes open-stage dance performances. *Open:* Tuesday to Sunday, 08.00–17.00 hrs. Entry charge. A Festival of Arts each June-July features *gamelan*, dances and traditional Balinese skills.

Central Market

This is across the stream from the original *Pasar Badung*. It is dark and hot, but filled with fascinating stalls. Go before 08.00 hours. Try typical snacks.

Temples

While Denpasar is a busy commercial centre, temple worship continues unperturbed. Many temples are hidden. Others, like **Pura Melanting**, the market temple, are obvious. Market vendors pause here to make offerings before work. Adjacent to the Bali Museum, **Pura Jagatnata** is dedicated to the supreme god, Ida Batara Sanghyang Widi Wasa. His coral

WHAT TO SEE ON BALI

Enticing displays of fruit and veg in Denpasar's Central Market

throne is mounted on a cosmic turtle and *naga* serpents. The best plan is not to devote too much time to temples in Denpasar as they are two a penny in the countryside.

Accommodation

You are unlikely to want to stay in Denpasar, but one hotel eases you nicely into Bali from overseas:

Natour Bali Hotel, Jalan Veteran 3, Denpasar 8011 (tel: (0361) 25681). Denpasar's original old downtown hotel, built in 1927, has a lingering colonial atmosphere. There are 74 large, plain rooms, a swimming pool and gardens. Moderate. Others are:

Adi Yasa, Jalan Nakula II. Within walking distance of the centre of town, it is pleasant, but no longer the traveller's refuge of

yesteryear. Cheap.

Hotel Denpasar, Jalan Diponegoro 103, Denpasar 80113 (tel: 28336). Cottage-style rooms. Guests mainly Indonesian. Moderate.

Food and Drink

At dusk *warung* (foodstalls) mushroom everywhere. **Pasar Senggol** ('Night Market', open 16.00–20.00 hours) is a good eating spot. Other centres are around bus and *bemo* stations and near the Wisata Theatre in Jalan Diponegoro. The latter sells delicious Muslim-made *satés* in rich, thick peanut sauce. Good Chinese food is to be had at **Restoran Puri Selua**, Jalan Gajahmada 16: more expensive, but air-conditioned. **Goyalli** is a cheap, fast-food restaurant with bar near the Indra Cinema. The **Bali Hotel** has an extensive Indonesian-European menu.

Nightlife

There is no Kuta-type entertainment. Evening dances *(kechak)* are performed at 18.30 hours nightly at the Art Centre. Go early to avoid coachloads. There is a female singer at the **Bali Hotel**.

Shopping

Denpasar sells crafts from all over Bali, but they are more expensive than in their places of origin. Crafts shops on Jalan Gajahmada sell paintings, carvings, etc. Above the Central Market, **Kumbasari Shopping Centre** sells handicrafts plus a lot of junk.

The government co-operative centre **Sanagraha Kriya Asta** (tel: (0361) 22942) is in Tohpati, on the road to Batubulan. It is

recommended for good quality woodcarving, painting, *batik* and silverware at fixed prices. Free transport is provided from and to your hotel in the Denpasar – Sanur – Kuta area. *Open:* Monday to Saturday 09.00–17.30 hrs.
Mega is a good shop next door with a branch at Jalan Gajahmada 36 in Denpasar.

Getting About
There are *bemo* services between the bus stations (see below) and Jalan Gajahmada, the main street. Self-drive is not recommended without a guide and remains a hair-raising experience. *Dokars*, pony-traps, are fun if you can find one. Dust, traffic and open drains make walking stressful.

Travelling On

Bus Stations
Denpasar has four main bus/*bemo* stations for travel to all parts of Bali:
Tegal (Kuta road) southern peninsula.
Ubung (Gilimanuk road) north and west. Main station for Java.
Kereneng (Tohpati road) east and central Bali.
Suci (central Denpasar) mainly to Benoa. Location of many Surabaya (Java) bus-lines and agents.
Other *bemo* terminals are (not much used by tourists):
Sanglah (south Denpasar) for Benoa Port.
Wangaya (north Denpasar) for travel north, to the Sangeh Monkey Forest.
If you are staying in Kuta-Legian, buy your bus-ticket for a journey on from Denpasar

from a local travel agent. The small extra charge saves hassle on the day.
Cost of your journey depends on the type of bus – *bemo*, micro-bus, or full-size vehicle. No fare on Bali should exceed Rp2,000. If buying from the bus company go early to obtain a window-seat. Many agents are located on Jalan Hasanudin in Denpasar.
Transfers between bus-stations are by *bemo*.

GIANYAR
southeastern Bali
A 20-minute drive from Denpasar, Gianyar District is famous for cottage industries, especially textiles (visitors may watch a sarong being woven), but the town itself is without interest.
About two miles (3km) north of the town is the **Pura Dalem** (temple of the dead), a good example of temple carving.

GILIMANUK
northwestern tip of Bali
This quiet old town is strung along Jalan Raya, the road to the ferry-crossing for Java. Few travellers stop and there are no tourist facilities … not even cold beer.
For anyone interested in natural history, the local mangrove swamps are rich in wildlife (see **Peace and Quiet** page 86), and the national park of Pulau Menjangan is off the coast near Gilimanuk. There is good diving off the island.

Accommodation/Food and Drink
'Jalak Putih' (the manager is

unsure of the name) is about six miles (10km) east on the Lovina Road. Eight simple, but spotless bungalows, with an exterior WC and shower (you pull a cork in a bucket) in an attractive site in a coconut plantation. The beach is black sand, but white beaches are accessible by *prahu*. There is good fishing, diving and windsurfing. Not well placed for general sightseeing, but one of the nicest spots on Bali. Italian-Indonesian menu. Licensed.

Ferry-Java. Buses connect with the steamer and car-ferry. The crossing takes 20 minutes and there are no formalities other than a ticket.

◆
GITGIT
northern Bali
The waterfall near the Singaraja – Bedugal road is a short detour from Gitgit village through lush paddy-fields. You can swim in the pool at the foot of the falls.

◆
GOA GAJAH
central Bali
The 'Elephant Cave' is a former Buddhist retreat, created in the 11th century. There are interior carvings, and a boy with a light will point out niches where the monks probably meditated. Admission charge. Hasslers are a nuisance.

◆
GOA LAWAH
East Coast, about 2 miles (3km) east of Klungkung
This is the 'Bat Cave', with thousands of bats and said to extend all the way to Besakih, 18 miles (30km) away. If you

stop, accept no 'gifts' of necklaces, etc, and take no pictures, unless you are prepared to pay. There are charges for parking and entry.

GUNUNG AGUNG see BESAKIH

◆◆◆
GUNUNG BATUR/ LAKE BATUR ✓

Central Mountains
This active volcano and crater lake lie at 5,630 feet (1,717m) in Bangli District, about four hours' drive from Denpasar. A branch road from Besakih is drivable, but badly pot-holed.
Lake Batur is a large, deep, green lake lying on the eastern side of the volcano in the outer crater rim. In the old days you had to walk or ride down by

horse from Penelokan (see page 63). The road is now tar, the macadam laid across the lava flow, making the 35-minute journey a thrilling roller-coaster ride. Sound your horn on the blind crests. There is a *bemo* service from Penelokan to the hot springs at Toya Bungkah. If you want to take to the water, Kedisan is the lake boat-terminal, with charter-boats (seating 12). Do not hire a dug-out and paddle yourself: Lake Batur is larger than it looks and storms are common. The best time for sightseeing is before 10.00 hours. Take a warm weatherproof coat.

Toya Bungkah (Tirtha) is the main tourist village on Lake Batur, a bleak settlement with

Batur volcano looms over the deep waters of Lake Batur

about a dozen *losmen,* built from volcanic rock. Local hot springs are a reviver if you have walked up Gunung Batur (see below). Locals are unfriendly and solitary women may not feel comfortable. Young people often make Toya Bungkah a base for climbing the volcano. See also **Kintamani** page 52.

Climbing Gunung Batur
Climbing Batur volcano is a different proposition to tackling Gunung Agung. The ascent is steep, but fit people should accomplish it without stress. It takes two to three hours to make the ascent to the 2,300-foot (700m) summit, and one and a half hours to descend. The most popular ascent is from Toya Bungkah; a guide is unnecessary. Choose one of the numerous well-indicated tracks and walk straight up. Take a sweater, although it is generally hot. Start by 06.00 hours, to be back for a late lunch. There are drinks stands on the way up if you are flagging. You can walk all around the crater rim to the point of descent at Purajati. Wisps of smoke indicate activity deep within the volcano – Batur last erupted in 1963. There are magnificent views on a clear day.

Accommodation
Balai Seni Toya Bungkah Art Centre. In a quiet spot, this is the only really pleasant place to stay – in detached bungalows with verandahs. It has a restaurant and library. Moderate.
Homestay Nyoman Mawa – 'Under the Volcano'. Near the

hot springs. A good base from which to climb Gunung Batur. Cheap.

Losmen Tirta Yatra. Above the hot springs, it attracts backpackers. Cheap.

Segara Homestay. With 29 modest rooms, above the lake, it is five minutes' walk from the boat-terminal. Has a restaurant. Cheap.

Food and Drink

'Under the Volcano' and **Nyoman Pangus Warung** provide local barbecued fish. No fancy meals. Beer available.

◆
GUNUNG KAWI

central Bali, 1 mile (1.5km) from Tampaksiring

These royal temples, or memorials, probably date from the 11th century. They are carved into cliffs with a river flowing between, and from one of Bali's most impressive sites. Legend says the carvings were completed in one night by a giant using his fingernails. The memorials – 10 in all – are among the earliest examples of Balinese art – Goa Gajah (see page 50) is another early site. You must climb hundreds of stairs to reach the complex.

◆
JATILUWIH

central Bali

The name means 'truly marvellous', and the views of rice-terraces justify it. The village is on the slopes of Gunung Batukau, one of Bali's highest peaks. As with most view-points in Bali, you have to gamble on clear weather when you are actually in the vicinity. Jatiluwih is off the tourist track.

KINTAMANI

Central Mountains

About four hours direct from Denpasar, or two hours south of Singaraja, Kintamani, Penelokan and Batur almost merge into a line of drab, wind-blown shops spread around the crater rim of Gunung Batur.

Kintamani is an important market town and fruit-growing area. Stay overnight to see sunrise and clearing mists over Lake Batur. There is a colourful market every three days, and an occasional performance of the strange *Sanghyang* trance dance (see page 98).

Accommodation

If you decide to stay, Kintamani has mercifully fewer touts than Penelokan (see page 63), but you may be disturbed by dogs ....or by cocks calling to each other in the caldera. Most *losmen* are too drab to recommend. Pay more for warmth and comfort at the **Hotel Puri Astini** which has private bathrooms, and excellent views and is moderately expensive. It is a detour of about half a mile (1km) off the main road to the north of Kintamani (signposted). Also in the northern end of town is the small, but friendly – for this area – **Hotel Miranda**. You will need warm clothes.

Food and Drink

You can eat in the hotels. **Miranda** has reasonable food and an open fire.

Shopping

Basketware and sarongs are genuine. Trash is in plentiful supply.

Good battles against Evil in the Kerta Gosa in Klungkung

Activities

Using Kintamani as a base, you can hike up Gunung Batur (see also page 51), or walk down to Lake Batur. A guide is unnecessary – but alone you will be pestered. Get up early to make a boat-trip to Trunyan village (see page 71).

Travelling On

A *bemo* shuttle service runs between Kintamani and Penelokan. Onward bus connections to Ubud/Gianyar-Denpasar and Singaraja.

◆◆◆
KLUNGKUNG

East Coast, 25 miles (40km) from Denpasar
Traffic is very bad until this point. Klungkung is a major road junction for Besakih and the northeast coast to Amlapura. While noisy and busy,

Klungkung is of considerable historic interest. Allow 40 minutes for leisurely sightseeing, or one and half hours if you include Kamasan. Klungkung was where descendants of the Majapahit Dynasty established a new kingdom after fleeing from Java. They first ruled from Gelgel, two miles (3km) south, and in 1710 moved to Klungkung. The old Gelgel dynasty ruled Bali for 600 years, when Klungkung was a flourishing arts centre. Like the rajas of Badung, the royal families of Klungkung committed suicide rather than capitulate to the Dutch. Most of Bali's nobility trace lineage to the 'Dewa Agung', the 'Great Lord' of Klungkung.
One of the main sights of the town is the **Kerta Gosa**. Surrounded by a moat, this Hall of Justice, stands on the right corner of the main intersection of streets in the town centre. The

WHAT TO SEE ON BALI

Balinese equivalent of the
Supreme Court, it settled
disputes not agreed at village
level. Defendants were judged
by three priests. Terrifying
panels depicting the horrors of
hell cover the walls and ceilings.
The murals are painted in
'wayang' style, with figures in
profile, the symbolism of right
and left equating Good and Evil.
Adjoining the Kerta Gosa is the
Bale Kambang or 'Floating
Pavilion'. Both buildings are a
reminder of the refined lifestyle
of the ancient kingdom of
Klungkung.
Open: daily. Parking and
admission charges.

Accommodation
You are unlikely to want to stay
in Klungkung. Among several
poor *losmen* is the **Ramayana
Palace**, on the road to
Amlapura. The rooms are very
simple. It is better to stay in
Ubud or Candi Dasa (see pages
74 and 44).

Food and Drink
Eat at the **Ramayana Palace**, or
the 'night market'.

Shopping
Several crafts shops are found
on Jalan Diponegoro: try No
241. Hawkers in the parking-lot
sell copies of paintings in the
Kerta Gosa. If you fancy the
style, you would do better to
buy one in Kamasan (see
below), where local artists
perpetuate old-style Gelgel
painting.

Side-Trips
Kamasan Village, 2½ miles
(4km) south, beyond Gelgel.
Here you can buy traditional
paintings – basically linear, in

browns, ochres and greens.
Purists searching for a painting
in Bali should consider these.
Kusamba, 15 minutes north.
This is a small fishing village on
a black sand beach. Roadside
scenery shows evidence of the
1963 eruption of Gunung
Agung, when lava buried
villages and fields. North of
Kusamba, a road leads to a salt-
panning village.

KRAMBITAN
*West Coast, 3.5 miles (6km)
inland from Klatingdukuh*
A detour of about six miles
(10km) from Tabanan,
Krambitan has ancient royal
palaces and traditionally
designed buildings, set off by
beautiful flowering shrubs. Off
the tourist track, but there is a
regular *bemo* service from
Tabanan.

KUTA (see also Legian)
*Southwest Coast, 10 minutes
from Denpasar Airport*
This is Bali's biggest beach
resort, with a strong Australian
bias. There are bars, cafés and
discos by the dozen; hotels by
the hundreds. Kuta is for young
ragers into surfing, drinking and
generally having a good time.
Backpackers like it, as
competition keeps prices down.
Other people regret they
bought a Kuta holiday. Kuta's
broad, white beach stretches
some six miles (10km) from
Tuban past Legian in the north.
Behind the main beach is a
large area of shops, art markets,
pubs, discos, travel agents and
rent-a-car-bike-jeep, or -tour.
Without traffic Kuta might be fun,

but walking is made an ordeal
by motorcycles and hustlers
importuning you to buy. Jalan
Legian – the route to Denpasar –
is perpetually blocked by traffic.
The best way to commute is via
the lanes, or *gangs*, although not
late at night. Drunken
Australians have given Kuta a
reputation for easy pickings.
Most incidents do not involve
Balinese.

Activities
Kuta has a splendid surf. The
best period is March–July.
Australian-trained Balinese
lifesavers patrol the beach
between the flags – there are
dangerous rips at the Legian
end. Joggers should get out
early before motorcyclists
begin riding up and down the
sand. There is an entry charge
for the main beach. You can buy
anything you want without
moving: drinks, fruits, snacks, T-
shirts, suntan oil, umbrellas. You
can even have a massage; and
women will also plait your hair.
Bargain as if your life depends
on it.

Accommodation
To enjoy Kuta, find a quiet hotel
near the beach and your
evening meal. Cheap *losmens*
are popular and advance
bookings are difficult.
Arena's Cottages, off Poppies
Lane. Small bungalows within
walking distance of the beach.
Cheap.
Ayu Beach Inn, Poppies Lane
(tel: (0361) 51664). Clean, airy
rooms. Cheap.
Mandara Cottages, (tel: (0361)
51775). The cottages are behind
the beach, in Kuta south-side.
Five minutes from the airport

*A swarm of hawkers settles around
a likely customer on Kuta Beach*

and 700 metres from shops.
Garden. Asian-European food.
Expensive.
Poppies, (tel: (0361) 51059). In
Poppies Lane, off Jalan Legian,
this is a little gem in central Kuta,
out of earshot of the din. Twenty
thatched cottages with fans, or
air conditioning. Clean, in
beautiful gardens around a
pool. You can walk to the beach.
Expensive. Poppies has some
cheaper cottages (without a
pool) near by.
Yasa Samudra, main beach (tel:
(0361) 51562). Forty rooms,
around a small pool. Good for
families. More expensive rooms
have air conditioning. Licensed
restaurant/bar.

Food and Drink
Like you should with
accommodation, walk around
and check restaurant menus.
Small, back-lane *warung*
(foodstalls) are most authentic.

Street-side restaurants offer 'international cuisine' with 'Down Under' specialities – roast dinners, jaffles, Vegemite! Shop around for bargain breakfasts: watered-down fruit juice, bacon and eggs, tea and toast. **Made's Warung** on Jalan Pantai Kuta (near Bemo Corner) has meals and snacks throughout the day and night. Walking to the beach from 'Bemo Corner', it is on the right: a good spot to people-watch. There are freshly baked croissants, etc at **Zas** on Jalan Legian, near the Hotel Legian Gardens.

Poppies Cottages offer peace and quiet in central Kuta

Where to eat dinner is more difficult to recommend. **Poppies** stylish garden restaurant has an international menu and is licensed. **Mini's Restaurant**, also on Jalan Legian serves seafood, but go early for a table. **Lenny's** on Jalan Pantai Kuta is another seafood restaurant, moderate, but inconsistent. **Dayu II**, opposite the Bar Casablanca, does steak and grilled fish.
Other tourist-type restaurants are found on Jalan Bakung Sari. **Gantina Baru** in this area specialises in *padang* food from West Sumatra. **Depot Viva** on Jalan Legian, open-roof, serves Indonesian food.
Kuta has a Kentucky-Fried Chicken, several pizza restaurants and ice-cream parlours.

Nightlife
It is unfair not to say that many young tourists find Kuta's night-life terrific. Others find it banal. **Pub-Crawls** are popular entertainment. Buses take increasingly drunken revellers on a local pub-tour. Tickets are sold by attractive Aussie sheilas in Kuta-Legian cafés. You can pay for pick-up and return to your hotel. Popular pubs are **Koala Blue**, **Bali Billabong**, and **Norm's Bar**. As the night wears on, drinking competitions and ladies wet T-shirt contests become more vulgar.
Some places have a 'happy hour' (18.00–22.00 hrs) when drinks are often 30 per cent less. Try the **Bali Balance Bar**. Or enjoy Kuta's famous sunset over cocktails in a beachfront hotel. Even the pricey **Bali**

Oberoi at Legian Beach discounts cocktails by 20 per cent between 18.30 and 19.30. **Discos**: what is flavour of the month at the time of writing may have fallen from favour now. Favourite discos of the moment are **Peanuts** and **Spotlight** on Jalan Legian; **Gado-Gado** near the beach at the Seminyak end; **Barong**; and **Double Six**. All feature loud Western pop music from 22.00 hours. Entrance fee includes a weak alcoholic beverage of your choice.

Shopping
Kuta is the fashion capital of Indonesia. Every second shop sells flashy 'beach style' clothing. Eclectic Balinese-Bondi designed T-shirts and board-shorts are bargain buys. Avoid stuff sold by hustlers as designs are not colourfast. So-called 'art markets' – lots of cheaper shops crowded together in a lane – flog down-market goods. Australians trying on leather jackets over their swimming costumes are one of Kuta's peculiar sights. Cassettes are good buys: **Top 10**, (Jalan Melasti 118, in Legian) is recommended. With clothes shops and money-changers, *quik-foto* print shops are prolific. Films are processed cheaply and quite reliably – **Bali Foto Centre**, on Jalan Pantai Kuta, is your best bet. Balinese arts and crafts are sold everywhere. Javanese hustling silver jewellery and fake watches are a nuisance. **Krishna Books** is a newsagent bookshop in Jalan Legian, with a good selection of travel books. Postcards and stamps are obtainable from a

kiosk in Jalan Legian. Check exchange rates at several different money-changers. **Post Office**: the main post office, 'Kantor Pas', is near the 'night market', off Jalan Raya Kuta.

Transport
Bemos. Start from 'Bemo Corner', to Denpasar. To Sanur, you must go via Denpasar and change from Tegal to Kereneng. Find companions to charter direct to Sanur. There is a service from the airport to Kuta. **Motorcycles**. Local youths earn their living taking pillion passengers between Kuta and Legian. You should wear a safety helmet. **Renting**. Many *losmen* have motorcycles, or push-bikes, for rent. They are also parked outside travel agents. Bicycles are best for local sightseeing. **Taxis** are the usual means of transport for visitors between airport and hotel (10-15 minutes' drive). Extra charge for luggage – negotiable.

◆
LEGIAN
Like Kuta, Legian was discovered by the 'flower people' of the 1960s. The two villages now merge – the *bemo* connection along Jalan Legian takes five minutes. The main street, Jalan Melasti, has Kuta-style travel agents, art markets and boutiques. There are plenty of hustlers too. North Legian, towards Seminyak, remains undeveloped jungle fringing the beach.

Accommodation
Check out *losmen* in the lanes on the north side of Jalan

Melasti. **Sri Beach Inn** in an orchid garden and **Janji Inn** in a coconut grove are possibilities, but there are several others that might fit your particular bill. If luxury is what you are after, try: **Bali Oberoi**, Jalan Kayu Aya, Legian (tel: (0361) 51061). Sophistication, quality and style summarise the 75-room Oberoi owned by the Indian hotel group. It has large air-conditioned bungalows with superb beds and sunken marble baths; de luxe Presidential villas have a private swimming pool. First class food. Complimentary daily shuttle service for shopping in Kuta. Quiet, beachfront location in Seminyak. Very Expensive.
Kul-Kul Resort, Jalan Pantai Kuta, Legian (tel: (0361) 52520). 77 rooms, 2-star. Moderate.
Legian Beach Hotel, Jalan Melasti, Legian (tel: (0361) 51715). Large tourist hotel, near the beach.

Nightlife
Most nightlife centres around Jalan Melasti. **Double Six** and **Gado Gado** are popular discos.

◆◆
LOVINA
North Coast, 6 miles (10km) west of Singaraja
Derived from 'love' and 'ina' which means pleasure, Lovina is the over-all name for a string of black sand beaches – Anturan, Kalibukbuk, Lovina, and others. It has a laid-back lifestyle with cheap, friendly hotels and activities, such as watersports, walking and cycling, making it ideal for families. However, younger travellers find it lacks ambience and it is certainly less

frenetic than Kuta-Legian. There is good diving and you can paddle out to the coral reef, or rent a *prahu*. Mountain-bikes can be hired.

Accommodation
Bali Lovina Beach Cottages, tel: (0362) 41385. Hotel with swimming pool/bar. On the beach. Moderate.
Banyualit Beach Inn, tel: (0362) 41889. Quiet, near the beach, it has clean rooms with large bathrooms and comfortable beds. Indonesian and seafood restaurant. Good value.
Baruna Beach Cottages, tel: (0362) 41252. The first hotel on the right on the road from Singaraja, it is on a delightful site, and has 24 rooms, good food and pleasant staff. Snorkelling and reef trips. Safe for children. Cheap.
Nirwana Cottages, tel: (0362) 41288. On a shady site right on beach. Attractive traditional style cottages. Cheap.

Food and Drink
Check roadside menus.
Harmoni restaurant in Anturan and **Khi Khi** restaurant (220 yards/200m from Nirwana Cottages) serve good, fresh seafood. The restaurants of **Baruna Beach Cottages** and **Banyualit Beach Inn** are also recommended.

Shopping and Nightlife
Penny Shop is the general store in central Lovina. Nightlife centres on small restaurant/bars.

Travelling On
There is a regular *bemo* service to Singaraja and several daily bus services to Gilimanuk.

◆◆◆
MAS
central Bali, 12 miles (20km) from Denpasar
Attractive wood-carving village on the road to Ubud. Many roadside workshops specialise in masks, including **I B Sutarja** (left side); **Balinese Pop Art** (left side); and for cats – **Mass Product Kt Astawa**.

Accommodation
Taman Harum Cottages, tel: 88511 ext 569. Situated next to Tantra Gallery, the Balinese style cottages have a view of rice-fields. There are sunken bath-tubs, and the super décor is by a local family of artists. Pool, restaurant/bar. Moderate.

◆◆
MENGWI
central Bali
The 17th-century royal temple complex of Pura Taman Ayun is

Competitors in the Negara bullock races ponder their chances

here in a beautiful setting surrounded by a moat. It was the state temple under a kingdom which ruled at Mengwi until 1891. Entry is through an elaborate gate. Visit the site in conjunction with Sangeh and the sacred 'Monkey Forest', (see page 64). Try the **Water Palace Restaurant** for lunch.

◆
NEGARA
59 miles (95km) from Denpasar
The largest town on the jungle-clad west coast, its annual highlight is the September/October bullock-races when pairs of decorated bullocks pull chariots around a rice-field (see page 108). To see this colourful and free spectacle, you should leave Denpasar by 06.00 hours, or stay overnight; tours from the main resorts can also be taken. Standard *losmen* line the main street in Negara. All are basic and none has air conditioning.

NUSA DUA
Southeast Coast, 30 minutes'
drive from Sanur
The southern peninsula is best
known for the huge,
meticulously planned Nusa Dua
tourist complex. It boasts a
2,500 seat convention centre
and some of Asia's finest and
most expensive, hotels –
Sheraton Nusa Indah, Sheraton
Lagoon, Grand Hyatt and the
deluxe Amanusa overlooking
the Bali Golf and Country Club.
The resort is well-manicured
and well patrolled by security. A
contrived Balinese atmosphere
pervades, but in reality you
could be anywhere…

Accommodation
There are no really cheap
rooms available. More
characteristic is: **Nusa Dua
Beach Hotel**, PO Box 1028,
Denpasar (tel: (361) 71210).
This is a huge hotel (450 rooms
and 27 suites) set in tropical
gardens and with bars, cocktail
lounges and restaurants. Dress
for dinner. There are evening
cultural shows as well as tennis,
squash, windsurfing and a
jogging track.

Shopping
There are expensive crafts and
clothes shops in the hotels. Art
Market shopping arcade
outside the gate of the hotel
compound. Local village is a
few minutes' walk away, with a
money-changer, general store,
quik-foto, etc.

Nightlife
Each hotel in Nusa Dua has a
programme of good evening
entertainment, (see **Culture**
pages 99–100).

Transport
There are hotel bus services to
Kuta-Legian. Public transport to
Nusa Dua is patchy, but there is
a *bemo* from Denpasar.

◆◆◆
NUSA PENIDA AND
NUSA LEMBONGAN ✓

These palm-fringed islands are
in the Badung Strait, 1½-2 hours
by motorboat from Padangbai,
Klungkung District. It makes a
fascinating day-trip, or Nusa
Lembongan has rustic
bungalows for a longer stay.
Package-tours depart from
Sanur. Independent travellers
should take a *bemo* to
Padangbai. Large motorboats
leave Padangbai daily from
08.00 hours every hour until

Supplies come by boat from Bali to Nusa Penida, once a penal colony

13.00 hours for Sampalan Mentigi, the islands' port. There are no facilities on board.

Nusa Penida

The larger of the two islands (77 square miles/200 sq km), it was a former penal colony for undesirables from the regency of Klungkung. In local mythology, it is the home of the ferocious giant Jero Gede Mecaling, the source of disease, disaster and evil magic. The island has white, powder-sand beaches shaded by coconut palms. The interior is arid and hilly. To walk from the landing to **Sampalan** takes 15 minutes. There are about 50 general stores, a post office and two banks which do not change foreign money, plus one or two crude restaurants. There is little to eat, brackish water and awful dogs.

Things to see on the island include **Pura Ped** and **Pura Batukuning** (to the east) temples and unspoiled villages. There is a basic government hotel which may be closed.

To reach Nusa Lembongan, catch a *bemo* to Toyapakeh (15 minutes). A pretty Muslim fishing village, it has two cafés. One has a WC and sells cold beer.

Bargain the cost of a motorised *prahu* to Nusa Lembongan with a local fisherman – you leave when the fisherman is ready. The trip takes 40 minutes.

Nusa Lembongan

This small island protected by coral reefs has white sand beaches, surfing and rustic game-fishing in the channel between it and Nusa Penida. There are no cars. You can walk from the landing site to a small village selling day-to-day requirements for the 2,000 inhabitants. Most people cultivate seaweed; at night they work by lamps when the lagoon twinkles like a 'night market'. Get up early to see the gardens at low tide. Laid out to dry, seaweed covers the island like a green carpet. It is sold to Japan, Singapore and France for processing into cosmetics and crackers.

Accommodation

This consists of basic *losmen* and bungalows. Stay on the beach rather than in the village. **Main Ski Inn**, **Wave Stay** and the **Nusa Lembongan**

Restaurant/Bungalows are recommended. They are simple and airy with exterior WC and showers. Island dress is casual.

Food and Drink
Eating is very limited. You can get *nasi goreng* and occasional fish at the **Nusa Lembongan Restaurant/Bungalows** and **Johnny's**. Cold soft drinks and beer are available. Take supplies if you plan to stay two or three days. A tourist hotel-restaurant is planned.

◆
PACUNG
central Bali
This small hillside village *en route* to Lake Bratan is recommended for a delightful hotel with comfortable rooms and spectacular views of the rice terraces, the **Pacung Cottages/Bar and Restaurant** (tel: (0361) 3839). It makes an excellent lunch stop; licensed

Two routes meet at the port of Padangbai: the Lombok car-ferry and the boat to Nusa Penida

and with a clean WC. Four miles (7km) away, there is a shuttle-bus service to Bedugal.

◆
PADANGBAI
East Coast, about 1¼ hours' drive from Denpasar
This small, scruffy Muslim port has no tourist facilities. It is the departure point for Nusa Penida-Lembongan (see page 60) and the car-ferry to Lombok. If you have an early sailing, stay over-night at the **Puri Buitan Hotel** at Balina Beach, 15 minutes' drive (see page 45). Local reefs offer good diving for experienced divers only.

◆
PEJENG
central Bali, on the Tampaksiring road
The village is known for the

Temple of the Moon – **Pura Penataran Sasih** – housing a vast bronze drum believed to be 1,000 years older than the Kingdom of Pejeng which came to an end in 1343. Legend says it came to earth as a fallen moon. The largest single cast drum in the world (it is about 10 feet/3m long), the great brass 'Moon Drum' is set high up in a pavilion. You can hardly see it. The **Museum Arkeologi** is just outside Pejeng.

PELIATAN
Bali heartland, ½ mile (1km) south of Ubud
Flourishing arts and crafts centre with one of the finest *gamelans* in Indonesia. Lots of galleries with industrious young artists. Popular with Westerners wanting to study Indonesian culture. Some *losmen* teach Balinese dancing.
Agung Rai Gallery is a huge art complex of *atap*-roof cottages (*atap* is stripped palm fronds). Each houses a different school of local art. Ask to see the owner's private collection of paintings by European artists. Dances and rehearsals can be seen in the **bale banjar** pavilion. Check times. There are Friday evening and Sunday morning rehearsals.

Accommodation
Stay here as an alternative to Ubud.
Homestay Puri Agung, Jalan Peliatan. Clean, quiet, Balinese-style bungalows. Owner teaches dancing. Cheap.
Mudita Inn, Jalan Peliatan.

Rooms with or without a bathroom, or *mandi* (see page 123). Family-run with home cooking. Cheap.

Food and Drink and Shopping
Eat at local *losmen* and village *warung*. See **Ubud**, page 74, for restaurant recommendations. Local paintings are the best buys for souvenir-hunters.

PENELOKAN
Central Mountains, 4 hours' drive from Denpasar
This is a popular tourist stop on the southern rim of Gunung Batur, at 4,757 feet (1,450m). Enjoyment of spectacular views is spoilt by hasslers. Do not leave your vehicle unattended. The town seethes with tourists and touts from mid-morning until 15.30 hours. To get here, if travelling by *bemo*, change at Gianyar, or Bangli.
You can walk from Penelokan around the crater rim and descend to the caldera and Lake Batur.

Accommodation
Basic *losmen*, which are tolerable on the coast, are miserable at cooler altitudes. Some have a fire – supply your own logs. People in Penelokan-Kintamani are very mercenary and charge what they think you can pay.
Losmen Gunawan hassle-free site on a spur with a great view of the volcano. Ask for an exterior room. Comfortable and friendly. Cheap.

Food and Drink
Tourist-style restaurants cater for coaches. The **Kintamani**

restaurants. Very popular.
Moderate.
Natour Sindhu Beach, Jalan
Danau Tondano 14, Sanur (tel:
(0361) 288351). First beach
front hotel in Sanur. Central.
Moderate.
Semawang Beach Inn, Jalan
Cemara Beach, Semawang-
Sanur (tel: (0361) 8619). In quiet
location, 220 yards (200m) from
the beach. Friendly staff, clean
rooms with air conditioning and
private bathroom. Ideal for two
friends sharing and
independent travellers. Bar.
Good value.
Surya Beach Cottages, Jalan

*Surya Beach Cottages enjoy the
seclusion of a private beach*

Mertasari, Semawang (tel:
(0361) 88833). Large,
comfortable Balinese-style
cottages set in gardens in
private beach location. Pleasant
atmosphere – no hustlers.
Facilities include watersports,
tennis, travel agent, baby sitter.
Ideal for families as well as
couples. Within walking
distance of Semawang village.
Moderate–expensive.
Tourist Beach Inn, Jalan Segara
Ayu, Sanur (tel: (0361) 88418).
Basic rooms; 110 yards/100
metres from the beach. Cheap.
Villa Bebek, corner of Jalan
Pengembak and Jalan
Mertasari, Semawang (tel:
(0361) 321507). Three villas
and one guest cottage in classic
Balinese style, sharing large
swimming pool. Each villa has
its own entrance, kitchen and
dining pavilion. Gorgeous but
expensive.
Villa Kesumasari II, Jalan
Kesumasari, Semawang-Sanur
(tel: (0361) 88371). Potentially
excellent, but spoiled by
barking dogs. Basic cottages on
the beach with private
bathrooms, air conditioning and
friendly staff. Cheap.

Food and Drink
There are Western-style bars
and restaurants on Jalan
Tanjung Sari. Bali-Indonesian
restaurants are few and far
between.
Istana Garden, Jalan Sindhu,
Sanur. Serves European and
Oriental food.
Jawa Barat, in Semawang, is a
cheap popular Indonesian
restaurant; licensed with helpful
staff. Menu in Indonesian.
Kesumasari Restaurant, on the

beach at Semawang, serves simple seafood-style meals. Licensed with lunch recommended.

Kulkul Restaurant, central Sanur, has a good reputation for seafood and local specialities.

La Taverna Hotel (see above). Attractive poolside restaurant with Indonesian buffet and à la carte western menu. Expectations of romantic dinners on the beach are spoiled by midges. 'Aussie breakfasts' are advertised by many places on Jalan Tanjung Sari. Most are spoilt by loud music and an odour of 'bar' from the night before. Shop No 3 in Sanur Art Market sells coffee and freshly baked croissants. You can even get lax and bagel.

Nightlife
Sanur does not have Kuta's rowdy nightlife, but Australian ravers are still found in discos such as **Sobek**. Life starts around 23.30 hours. The Hyatt's **Mata Hari** disco attracts sophisticates.

Shopping
Most shops in Sanur are a rip-off, but if you have not shopped in Mas-Ubud, try **Ucok Antiques** for primitive art, and the gallery **Eurasia Bali**; both are near the Bali Hyatt. There are bookshops, money-changers and pharmacies on 'Sanur Beach Street'.

Tours
Sanur-Semawang is the best base for sightseeing in Bali. Shop around for dance-tickets and tours.

You can take a day-trip to **Serangan Island** or 'Turtle Island', south of Sanur, close to Benoa harbour. The island looks charming from the shore, but it is a tourist trap. If you want to go there, wait until low-tide when you can walk out. There are miserable turtle pens, and a temple, Pura Sakenan.

SINGARAJA
North Coast, 53 miles (85km) from Denpasar

This was the old Dutch capital and a major port in colonial times. The present population is about 16,000. It is now a busy market town counting many different religious groups – Muslim, Chinese, Buddhist and Hindu. Little Western influence remains except for vestiges of 19th-century colonial buildings. You should visit the old **harbour area** with its monument to independence, and the **Gedong Kirtya** at the eastern end of Jalan Veteran, a historical library with over 3,000 old Balinese manuscripts inscribed on *lontar* palm-leaf. *Open:* 08.00 hours Tuesday to Saturday, but make an appointment as this is a working library, not merely a tourist attraction.

Also worth a look is the market square, with its rows of Chinese shops.

Hand-weaving is the local craft, and you can look into a factory, just behind the library, to see it being done.

Another attraction is the bullock races held after harvest (see page 108). For details check with the Tourist Office (tel: (0362) 21142).

The old Dutch influence is reflected in the 19th-century architecture of Singaraja, once the colonial capital

Accommodation
There are hotels in the town, mostly on Jalan JA Yani, but it is more pleasant to stay at Lovina (see page 58). Recommended in Singaraja is:
Hotel Duta Karya, 59 Jalan JA Yani (tel: 21467). Convenient to Garuda office and local *bemo* station, it has spotless rooms with private bathrooms. Moderate.

Food and Drink
There are good eating-places around **Pasar Mumbil** market on Jalan JA Yani, and recommended Chinese food at the oddly named **Restaurant Gandhi** (fairly expensive).

Shopping
Best buys are hand-woven sarongs and silverware from the local village of Baratan.

Travelling On
Buses and mini-buses to Denpasar depart half-hourly

(06.00–16.00 hours) from Stasion Banyusari. Singaraja is the major transport terminal for the north and buses leave for everywhere, including overland to Java-Surabaya. Ticket offices are at the junction of Jalan JA Yani and Jalan Diponegoro.

SUKAWATI
East Coast 9 miles (15km) north of Denpasar
In this dirty market town, shops along the main road sell wind-chimes and woven hats, bags, mats, etc. Coach tours stop at the 'Sukawati Art Market' – in a huge, cramped, poorly lit complex selling a lot of trash compared to the well-made artefacts in Mas-Ubud. You get what you pay for.

TABANAN
southwest Bali, en route to Negara, 46 miles (74km) northwest
With Badung and Gianyar, the district of Tabanan forms the

island's richest rice-belt.
Tabanan township, like other
former capitals, has been
overtaken by Denpasar. It has
little of interest although it is
historically associated with
gamelan orchestras. Mario, the
famous exponent of pre-war
classic dance, came from here.
Subak Museum covers the
history of rice cultivation,
irrigation and the *subak* (rice-
growers' association) system.
Open: daily from 08.00 hrs.
An animal market is held every
three days in Kediri, a village
near Tabanan. If you have
wheels, picturesque side-roads
in Tabanan region often end at
deserted surfing beaches. The
coast here is not developed for
tourism.

TAMPAKSIRING
*central Bali, 23 miles (37km)
from Denpasar*
The town is known for the **Tirta
Empul** temple where the
Pakrisan river bubbles up in
ancient baths. An inscription
indicates it has been a sacred
site since AD962. People travel
from all over Bali to bathe in the
crystal clear water. Soekarno
had a hill-top palace built so he
could watch them. Unfortunately,
Tampaksiring has become a
major hawker site. To reach the
temple, you have to walk down
a long path lined with stalls
selling everything from hand-
crocheted tablecloths to turtle
shells. Expensive drinks and
snacks are available. Avoid
going at weekends.

Getting There
Take a *bemo* from Denpasar
and change at Gianyar. Most

tours include Tampaksiring *en
route* to Lake Batur. There is
parking.

TANAH LOT
*Southwest Coast, about 1 hour's
drive from Denpasar*
A detour at Kediri off the west
coast road to Gilimanuk, Tanah
Lot is Bali's best known sea-
temple, commanding equal
reverence to the mountain
shrines. Like Ulu Watu (see
page 76) it is associated with
the 16th-century priest Nirartha.
Legend says a serpent dwells
inside one of the shrines, but is
discreetly left undisturbed.
Tanah Lot is built on a
honeycombed rock carved by
the tides. At low tide, you can
cross to the temple, where a
priest demands a donation. Like
Tampaksiring, Tanah Lot is
central to hard-sell
commercialism. Again you must
run the gauntlet of souvenir
stalls and hawkers, on the path
down to the sea. The site is
especially crowded with tourist
buses at sunset. To avoid
everyone go on an early
morning high tide.

Accommodation
Le Meridien Bali opening mid-
1995 with 265 deluxe rooms.

Transport
There is no regular *bemo*
service. You can be dropped,
but getting back is difficult.
There are tours visiting Tanah
Lot from Kuta.

TENGANAN
*East Coast, inland from Candi
Dasa*
Like Trunyan (see page 71), a

WHAT TO SEE ON BALI

Bali Aga village, having friendlier inhabitants. It is a walled village with a typical town square shaded by a huge banyan tree. Simple restaurants sell snacks and drinks. Tenganan's 180 or so families follow Bali Aga traditions dating from before the Majapahit invasion of Bali. They do not marry outside, and celebrate ancient marriage customs. *Kawin pandan* is a yearly event, when a young man throws a flower over a wall and the girl who catches it (even if she is the ugliest girl in Tenganan) is his bride. At the *Usaba sambah*, (an annual festival in June or July) there are processions and boxing contests between men with their fists wrapped in pandanus leaves. The *gamelan selunding*, a sacred, archaic orchestra, performs in Tenganan once a month. Tenganan is renowned for double-*ikat* cloth, in which warp and weft are dyed separately before the fabric is woven. It has a typically dark terracotta background with white and yellow patterns. The cloths are used in teeth-filing ceremonies, at weddings and to bury the dead. Only about six families still know the old *ikat*-process, and Tenganan is the only place in Indonesia where it is done.

Shopping

Local craft products are double-*ikat* and other woven fabrics, shawls, woven baskets, bamboo musical instruments and palm-leaf books. Check a few different shops and houses for quality, and price.

Getting There

There is a *bemo* from Candi Dasa. It is a detour of about 1¾ miles (3km) uphill (but easy walking) off the main road, south. If you do not want to walk, motorcyclists offer pillion rides up (for a fee). Or you can rent a bicycle in Candi Dasa and freewheel back down.

◆◆◆
TIRTAGANGGA ✓

East Coast, 15 minutes' drive from Candi Dasa

This is one of the best spots to relax in Bali with a tranquil site and walks through stunning rice-terraces. It is known for an Indian-style water palace with statues, fountains, lily-ponds, built in 1947 by the water-loving raja of Ujung (see page 76). There is a clean public swimming pool and a *warung* at the gate. There are no banking facilities, so bring what money you may need – very little is necessary beyond the charge for entry to the water palace.

Accommodation

This is limited to *losmen*. **Tirta Ayu Home Stay** is within the water palace complex. It consists of four clean, basic bungalows, superb for solitary travellers. A pleasant restaurant overlooks the tanks. Good fish. Cheap.

Travelling On

A *bemo* runs into Amlapura. Buses continue on to Singaraja – there is a bus-stop outside the water palace. Hitchiking up the northeast coast is usually simple as there are far fewer tourists than in other parts of Bali. Hitchhikers tend to be treated more like locals.

TOYA BUNGKAH, see
GUNUNG BATUR

◆◆◆
TRUNYAN
on Lake Batur
Accessible generally by boat,
the village is inhabited
exclusively by an ethnic tribe
with ancestral links predating
the Majapahit invasion. Dark,
taciturn folk, the Bali Aga are
culturally as well as ethnically
different to the Balinese. The
dead are not cremated.
Wrapped in a shroud, a corpse
is left in a bamboo cage. If it has
not disappeared within a few
weeks, it is unceremoniously
tossed into the forest. Skulls,
bones and old coins are
scattered about the clearing by
the lake – 1¾ miles (3km) from

*The Trunyan people are a race
apart from the Balinese, and have
their own customs and practices*

the village. Other customs are
kept secret. Bali's largest statue
of Ratu Gede Pancering – 13
feet (4m) high – guardian of
Trunyan, is hidden.
Trunyan is not a place to stay, as
there are primitive facilities only
in the village. Visit is by
donation – be prepared for
extravagant demands from the
people. Fish-hooks are
appreciated.
See also **Tenganan** and **Gunung
Batur** (pages 69 and 50).

◆◆
TULAMBEN
on the northeast coastal road
The village is reached via a
spectacular drive from
Tirtagangga. Terraced rice-
fields alternate with barren lava
flows and the road skirts the
base of Gunung Agung. People
visit Tulamben for the diving off
accessible coral reefs.

WHAT TO SEE ON BALI

The wreck of a US Liberty ship, torpedoed in 1942, lies one mile (1.5km) offshore at a depth of 20-98 feet (6-30m). The *losmen* (see **Accommodation** below) organises diving packages including airport transfers.

Accommodation
Paradise Palm Beach Bungalows, PO Box 31, Amlapura. 10 small, comfortable bungalows on the rocky beach. Friendly atmosphere. Small, licensed restaurant. Unsuitable for young children.

◆◆◆
UBUD ✓

south-central Bali
An hour's drive from the airport

Rice fields near Ubud, a haven of tranquillity and centre of culture

and 21 miles (34km) from Kuta, Ubud is the perfect foil to 'sun 'n surf'. With Mas, and surrounding hamlets, Ubud is the cultural heart of Bali. The island's most skilled wood-carvers, painters, musicians, dancers and artists live here. There are schools where you, too, can study dancing and mask-making. Foreign artists such as Rudolf Bonnet and Walter Spies were residents of Ubud between the wars and there is still a small, semi-permanent community of Western artists. Culture apart, Ubud is a base for enchanting walks. There is nowhere like it: do not dismiss it in a few hours' visit.

Sightseeing
At first sight the town centre gives the impression of being a rural Kuta. To an extent this is true, but Ubud manages to strike a balance between nature and commercialism. Money-changers, galleries, souvenir shops – and even a supermarket – line its long, often muddy main street. Signs also advertise bicycles, *barong* dances and cheap tours. In the centre is a temple and tranquil lotus garden. Walk from the post office to Murni's Warung by the Campuhan bridge and back.
Lotus Garden. A lotus-choked pond set in peaceful grounds, it is perfect for contemplation.
Museum Puri Lukisan. From the gardens, cross the river gully and climb the hill to reach Ubud's fine arts museum. Established in 1956, the museum traces the evolution of local art from early masters to

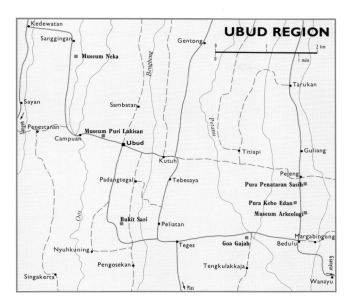

the so-called 'young artists',
who evolved a new style of
painting in the 1960s. Museum
and gardens are both in need of
upkeep.
Open: daily 08.00–16.00 hrs.
Museum Neka. To reach it, turn
right beyond the suspension
bridge – about 30 minutes'
walk. The museum exhibits
modern art produced by
Balinese and other Indonesian
artists, and with works by
Western artists who painted in
Bali, among them Theo Meier,
Donald Friend, Arie Smit and
Hans Snel.
Open: daily 08.30–17.00 hrs.

Local Walks
Ubud and its environs is a
walker's paradise of deep
jungle-clad river gorges and
lush rice-fields. Walking is

entirely safe. Should you
become lost, hit the main road
and stop a passing *bemo*. Just
1¾ miles (3km) outside Ubud,
the Ananda Cottages are an
ideal base (see below under
Accommodation). Walk from
here to Campuhan and
Penestanan, one of the main
villages of the 'young artists'.
You will pass other small hotels
hidden in the rice fields.
**Wanara Wana (Monkey Forest
Road) Walk**. This is easy to
follow, straight out of central
Ubud. It is lined with *losmen* and
shops, but further along you
enter the cool forest. Be careful
of monkeys. You can walk on to
Peliatan (see page 63). Be a
little cautious of young men
lurking along the Monkey
Forest Road – this is Ubud's
worst area for thieving.

To Pejeng. A trail beyond the T-junction takes you via a river gorge to Pejeng. *En route* you pass the **Pura Kebo Edan**, or buffalo temple. Balinese humour gives the buffalo statue six penises. For **Pejeng temple**, see page 62.

Bentuyung Walk. This is a loop of about five miles (8km) through beautiful rural scenery. Return via Kutuh reaching the tarmac near Peliatan. Locals are used to walkers and most understand sufficient English to point you in the right direction.

Accommodation

Ubud counts some of the nicest accommodation in Bali. Hotels and *losmen* are scattered liberally in and around the town. Villages such as Penestanan and Peliatan also have places to stay. The Monkey Forest Road has dozens of cheap homestays. Some hotels are literally planted in the rice fields.

Ananda Cottages, Banjar Kutuh Kedewatan, Ubud (no telephone). Five minutes by taxi from Ubud, 39 cottages, sunk in a gorgeous location surrounded by rice fields. Pool and rural walks. Licensed restaurant, pleasant staff. Moderate.

Cahaya Dewata Country Villas, Kedewatan (tel: (0361) 95171). Near the Museum Neka 1¾ miles, (3km) from Ubud – 22 spacious rooms overlooking the Ayung River Valley. Some steep climbs for older guests. Ideal for couples. Pool and licensed restaurant. Western and Indonesian breakfasts – excellent black rice with wine and coconut milk. Very quiet. Courtesy car to Ubud.

Moderate tariff.

Kori Agung Bungalows, PO Box 10, Ubud. In the heart of the rice fields at Campuan-Ubud. Comfortable and friendly, with a refrigerator in each room, but no hot water. Hard to reach if you have lots of luggage. Great value.

Kupu Kupu Barong (tel: (0361) 95470). Luxurious 2-storey Balinese bungalows overlooking the Sayan Valley. Pool and licensed restaurant. Up to three children to 16 years may share with two adults. Free bus-service to Ubud. Views better than the food. Expensive.

Murni's Bungalows by the Campuhan bridge. Comfortable, quiet and convenient to central Ubud. Meal service from Murni's Warung (see **Food and Drink** below). Moderate.

Puri Saraswati Bungalows, Jalan Ibu Raka Arimas (tel: (0361) 95164). In central Ubud, next to the Lotus Gardens, with comfortable rooms. You have to get used to the sound of rakes scraping up fallen frangipani. Popular, convenient and moderately-priced.

Wisata Cottages, Campuan, 1¼ miles (2km) from Ubud – 19 clean, simple cottages overlooking farmland. Swimming, table tennis. No charge for up to two children under 12 with parents. Cheap.

Food and Drink

Market stalls serve cheap food. Ubud has a limited number of restaurants.

Han Snel's Garden Restaurant. Jungle sounds in central Ubud. Very good Indonesian food.

Views of the Ayung River Valley are had from the Cahaya Dewata Country Villas, Ubud

Closed Sunday.
Lotus Café, just west of the *bemo* station, is a relaxed restaurant overlooking the Lotus Garden. Western-style dishes and snacks – pasta, cheesecake, crêpes, etc – are served. Always crowded. Ideal for families. Licensed.
Murni's Warung, by the Campuhan bridge, has Western and Indonesian food. Very pleasant, very popular, very good value. Licensed. Closed Wednesday.
Suci Inn, on the road opposite Monkey Forest Road, offers good homestyle Balinese meals. Order in advance. Authentic setting with *gamelan* music.

Nightlife
This is not what Ubud is about and remains low-key. Local dance performances are advertised.

Shopping
Ubud has many shops, galleries and a somewhat trashy market. Check out the small shops along the Monkey Forest Road. Good places to look for paintings are on the road to the Museum Neka. Visit other artists' villages before you buy.
W Barwa Painter-Workshop is a large roadside gallery in Peliatan. Many talented artists lived in the Padangtegal area – the late Australian painter Donald Friend worked here. Expect to pay £300-£400 ($500) upwards for anything of merit.

Travelling On
Bali's most popular destination, Ubud is well served by public transport. The *bemo* station is beside the cinema. Bicycles may be hired. There is an onward bus service to

Penelokan-Lake Batur and
Gianyar-East Coast.

◆◆
UJUNG
East Coast
Within walking distance of
Amlapura is the water palace
built in 1921 by Anak Agung
Anglurah, last ruler of
Karangasem (see also
Tirtagangga, page 70), a place
of crumbling pavilions, reed-
choked moats, and canals.
Walk, or drive, over the hill to a
picturesque Muslim fishing
village with black sand beach.
The road ends six miles (10km)
further north. There is no tourist
development. An irregular
bemo service runs from

*The impressive view from Ulu
Watu, famous for boardriding*

Amlapura. Take food and drink
for a swim/picnic.

◆◆◆
ULU WATU
*southwest coast of Bukit-Nusa
Dua peninsula*
The Pura Ulu Watu sea-temple is
about 30 minutes' drive from the
Nusa Dua-Kuta road junction.
Legend says the Pura Ulu Watu
is a ship turned to stone. It is a
hot climb up to the temple,
dramatically perched on the
edge of a high cliff. Entry to the
courtyard is forbidden. Be
careful of resident monkeys.
Turquoise surf lashing the cliffs
gives one of Bali's best views.

Surfing
True-blue boardriders surf at
Ulu Watu which has about six
different breaks with a big swell.
'Inside Corner' and the 'Peak'
are most commonly surfed, but
you need experience. To reach
the beach, take the track
marked 'Sulaban Beach' on the
right before Ulu Watu.
Several *warung* cater to the
exclusively young, bronzed
surfing crowd.

◆◆
YEH SANIH
*north coast road, 9 miles (15km)
east of Singaraja*
This is an attractive coastal centre
with freshwater pools and
gardens. **Pura Taman Manik Mas**
temple overlooks the springs.

Accommodation
Bungalow Puri Sanih. Garden-
style within the springs
complex. Cheap.
Yeh Sanih Seaside Cottages.
Picturesque site overlooking the
ocean. Clean, quiet and
moderately priced.

PEACE AND QUIET

Countryside and Wildlife on Bali and Java

by Paul Sterry

Bali and Java can justifiably claim to be paradise islands. Although Bali in particular has suffered as a result of growing tourism as well as an increase in its own population, both still retain a strange beauty that owes as much to their culture and religion as it does to the landscape.

In these highly populated islands, wildlife and the environment have often had to take second place to the needs of the human population. However, many wonderful wilderness areas of forested volcanic peaks, swamps and coast still remain, full of wildlife. To the credit of the islands, often aided by the World Wide Fund for Nature, some of the best areas are now reserves or national parks.

When the 19th-century naturalist Sir Alfred Wallace visited Indonesia, he noted the unusual geographical affiliations of the region's plants and animals. On islands to the west of Bali, the wildlife is essentially tropical Asian in origin while to the east, the ties are with Australia. In past times, the deep Lombok Straits proved a physical barrier to the spread of plants and animals from west to east. Hence Bali and Java, west of the so-called Wallace Line, have more than twice as many breeding bird species as adjacent Lombok, and a completely different flora.

Bali

Bali is a land of rolling landscapes where everything somehow seems in place. Tradition and religion seemingly pervade the whole of Balinese life. Man's influence not only manifests itself in temples and shrines, but is also strongly felt in the countryside where terraced rice fields are *the* dominant feature, covering most of the southern half of the island.

Yet there is another more natural side of Bali. It is an island of stunning beaches, mangroves, rolling hills and towering, forested mountains. The northern half of the island, dominated by a chain of volcanic peaks, is the region least affected by man, but natural history interest can be found almost anywhere if you look.

The whole of the Indonesian region is dominated by volcanoes, and eruptions – generally on a minor scale – are by no means a rare occurrence. One of the world's most famous volcanoes, Krakatau, lies near by off the west coast of Java. When it erupted in 1883, it killed tens of thousands of people and affected the world's climate. Nowadays, the volcanic peaks of northern Bali are mostly dormant, but one, Gunung Batur, occasionally rumbles and fumes. Intrepid visitors can trek to the summit from Toya Bungkah (see page 51).

The forested slopes of the northern mountains are good for wildlife, if a little difficult to explore. Exotic birds such as

PEACE AND QUIET

A lar gibbon – look out for them in Cibodas National Park, west Java

Bali Barat National Park

Bali Barat Taman Nasional lies in the Buleleng district of Bali in the far northwest of the island. The ancient volcanic peaks and dense, tropical monsoon forests which cloak the steep slopes of the reserve are characteristic of much of northern Bali and harbour rich delights for visiting naturalists. Bali Barat lies near Gilimanuk, Bali's westernmost ferry port, and can be reached from Denpasar by travelling along the main western road via Antosari and Negara.

Although Bali Barat is rich in all sorts of wildlife, it is most famous for its Bali starlings, sometimes also called Rothschild's minas. The reserve is their last remaining stronghold and the world population of these beautiful birds is put at no more than a few hundred strong. Part of the reason for their decline is a reduction in suitable breeding habitat, in particular the felling for firewood by local people of the dead acacia trees in which they prefer to nest. The effects of this activity are felt even within the park itself. Fortunately, a nest-box programme may help the starling's plight.

Bali Barat Taman Nasional is best explored early in the morning before temperatures begin to soar and when many of the creatures are at their most active. Colourful butterflies dance in the dappled light along forest rides and paths. Less conspicuous are the park's more retiring inhabitants, such as wild boar, tree shrews, several species of snakes and

hornbills, flowerpeckers, minivets, sunbirds and coucals abound and mammals such as leaf monkeys and macaques may also be seen. The further west you travel, the wilder the country becomes.

Closer to Denpasar, the 'Monkey Forest' near Ubud offers close views of tame macaques and attracts large numbers of visitors. Not far from the capital, paddy fields are fished by kingfishers, storks and herons, while edible nest swiftlets hawk overhead for insects. Nearby mangroves are the haunt of crabs and mudskippers, and are feeding grounds for herons and white-browed crakes and waders such as red-necked stints, long-toed stints, Terek sandpipers, wandering tattlers and eastern curlews.

banded pittas. Like all members of this family of birds, banded pittas are shy and are most frequently seen either by chance or by patient and quiet observation of the undergrowth. Many of the other birds of Bali Barat, such as green junglefowl, coppersmith barbets and pied imperial pigeons are more obvious, but flowerpeckers and sunbirds are so active that they yield only tantalisingly brief views.

By way of contrast to the forests of Bali Barat, the nearby coasts are well worth exploring. Mangrove swamps near Gilimanuk are rich in fiddler crabs, mudskippers, herons and kingfishers, while the marine reserve at Pulau Menjangan has beautifully clear water and is good for snorkelling.

You need sharp eyes to see leaf insects like this – after all, they are designed not to be seen

Cibodas National Park

Much of the natural jungle which once cloaked west Java has long since disappeared, being replaced by rice fields and small-scale agriculture. It is refreshing, therefore, to find less than 60 miles (100km) from Jakarta some fine areas of unspoilt habitat.

Cibodas Taman Nasional protects wonderful, pristine areas of rainforest together with a seemingly endless variety of plants and animals.

The park's proximity to the capital means that it can be visited on a day trip with an early start. However, to get the most from the area and in order to be there at dawn – the best time of day for views and observing wildlife – consider staying overnight. To reach Cibodas, travel south from Jakarta to Bogor and then southeast for about six miles (10km).

Cibodas National Park was originally set aside to protect some of Java's more unusual forest plants. The Botanic Gardens, which mark the entrance to the park, are a reminder of this. The birdlife is also good, with most, if not all, of Java's endemic species being found, plus numerous insects and mammals.

Permits and maps can be obtained from the Forestry Office in the gardens and to explore the park properly, visitors need to be reasonably fit. The gardens lie at around 4,000 feet (1,220m) and from here trails lead through the rainforest past streams, pools and waterfalls. The ultimate

PEACE AND QUIET

destination is the summit of the volcanic Gunung Gede and *en route* the forest grades into cloud forest and finally low scrub at the highest altitudes. To hike to the summit and back might take 15 hours but it is by no means necessary to undertake this to enjoy the wildlife.

Orchids and other epiphytic plants festoon the trees and tree ferns grow to enormous sizes. Large butterflies fly among the canopies of the immense trees, tree shrews can sometimes be seen and gibbons and long-tailed macaques are often noisy and conspicuous. The birdlife is varied but can be frustratingly difficult to see. The dappled light and dense foliage often conspire to make accurate identification impossible, but azure nuthatch, pygmy tit, black drongo, pink-necked fruit dove and mountain leaf warbler are

*Nice bird, shame about the name –
this is a black drongo*

BALI AND JAVA - WILDLIFE

among the more exotic species that may be encountered.

Ujung Kulon National Park

Lying on the far western tip of Java, Ujung Kulon Taman Nasional is one of the most attractive and unspoilt parts of the whole island. The dense, tropical forest is the main attraction of the reserve but it also boasts marshes and meadows, beautiful waterfalls and stunning beaches and coral reefs. Access and observation is made easy by a network of trails and paths and observation towers and the variety of wildlife to be found in Ujung Kulon is remarkable. Above all else, one creature in particular has made the reserve famous: it is the last haunt of the Javan rhino which undoubtedly would be extinct were it not for this national park.

Although Ujung Kulon is linked to mainland Java by a narrow isthmus, the swampy nature of this land-bridge effectively isolates the park. Access into and out of Ujung Kulon is by

boat from nearby Labuhan
where permits can also be
obtained from the Forestry
Office. Organised tours also
operate out of Labuhan which
may provide visitors who have
a limited amount of time with
the best opportunities for
seeing the rhinos.
Although people commonly
associate rhinos with open
grasslands, the preferred
habitat of the Javan rhino is the
dense jungle where it feeds on
leaves and shoots. Males have a
single, short horn which is
absent in the females. Despite
their size, the animals are
surprisingly unobstrusive in the
forest. They are easier to see
when they visit nearby beaches
and wallows. Other mammals
inhabiting Ujung Kulon are
barking deer, sambur, gibbons,
wild pigs and wild oxen.
The loud, trumpeting calls of
green peafowls herald the
dawn, which is undoubtedly the
best time of day for walking and
birdwatching. Search the
forests for ashy drongos,
babblers, woodpeckers and

flycatchers. On the beaches
you will see waders, terns,
herons and kingfishers.
The volcanic island of Krakatau,
which erupted in 1883 and
devastated the region, lies a
short distance to the west of
Ujung Kulon. Boat trips can be
arranged in Labuhan, about 60
miles (100km from Jakarta), and
visitors are constantly struck by
the amount of plant and animal
life that has colonised the island
in such a relatively short time.

East Java
Probably because of the
distance from the capital, East
Java is more rural than many
parts of the island. It can be
reached either by a long drive
from Jakarta or by ferry from
Gilimanuk on Bali. A region of
comparatively low and very
seasonal rains, east Java has a
predominance of plantations,
but there are still considerable
areas of natural forest left.
Almost anywhere that looks
unspoilt will harbour wildlife but
three areas in particular are
especially good: Meru Betiri

PEACE AND QUIET

Taman Nasional still harbours a few Javan tigers, Baluran Taman Nasional has herds of game animals and Banyuwangi Suaka Margasatwa (Banyuwangi Selatan Reserve) is a remote area of monsoon forest. See map on pages 80–1 for location of reserves.

Meru Betiri Taman Nasional lies on the southern coast of east Java near Sukamade. Hills rise steeply from the sea to an altitude of over 3,000 feet (900m) and these are cloaked in dense forests. Without doubt, the most spectacular plant to be found here is a species of rafflesia, which produces one of the largest but most elusive flowers in the world. Equally spectacular are the reserve's Javan tigers but these are now so rare that visitors are unlikely to see one. Forest birds such as hornbills, jungle-babblers and white-eyes are more easily seen as are the squirrels, long-tailed macaques and leaf monkeys.

Baluran Taman Nasional, in the northeast of Java is an area of monsoon forests, swampy marsh and grassland on the shores of the Bali Straits and overlooked by the volcanic cone of Gunung Baluran. Excellent views can be had of herds of wild oxen, wild pigs, wild dogs (dholes) and sambar deer in the open country. As for birds, marshlands are favoured by stork-billed kingfishers and milky storks, while the forest margins are the haunt of green peafowl, ashy drongos, rufous-winged buzzards and many more.

Banyuwangi Suaka Margasatwa lies on the Blambangan peninsula in the southeast corner of east Java. The comparative inaccessibility of the reserve is the key to the survival of its monsoon forests and pristine beaches. Waders, herons, terns and frigatebirds can be seen around the coast, where some of the sandy beaches are visited by nesting turtles. The open forests have leaf monkeys, wild dogs, wild pigs and numerous species of birds.

Rainforests

Rainforests are found throughout the tropics from South America to Africa and from Australia to Southeast Asia. In these regions the rainfall is high, generally over 100 inches (2,540mm) a year and the temperatures are hot, which means the humidity remains constantly high, making an environment suitable for tropical rainforests to thrive. The climate of the rainforests remains largely stable throughout the year although those of Indonesia, being subject to the monsoon rains, have slightly more seasonal variation than rainforest regions elsewhere. With stability comes diversity in the plants and animals. Even the trees are diverse. Unlike areas of temperate forest which comprise maybe three or four species in uniform stands, a good area of primary rainforest (one which has not previously been felled) could be expected to harbour more than 300 species of tree in just a few square kilometres.

Only a fraction of west Java's once widespread rainforest survives today

Although most parts of Bali and Java are too dry (by tropical standards) for rainforest to grow, much of western Java has a suitable climate. Mountain chains and volcanic peaks elsewhere also provide localised areas of high rainfall suitable for this habitat. One of the first things to strike people as they enter the world of the rainforest is the size and scale of everything. The trees are immense, supported by spreading buttress roots, and give the overall impression of a high, vaulted ceiling. Because little light penetrates the dense leaf canopy high above, many smaller plants choose to grow not at ground level but up in the tree tops. Hundreds of species of orchids and other epiphytic plants grow attached to branches and have aerial roots which never touch the ground. The soils are shallow and low in nutrients, most of what is available being efficiently recycled. Some plants supplement their nutrient intake in unusual ways: pitcher plants catch insects in water traps while the giant rafflesia feeds on the sap of vines. As elsewhere in the world, Java's rainforests have been largely felled or severely reduced in size although a few areas are protected by national parks or reserves. This destruction is now viewed by many as a tragic loss, not only for future generations but also because of the rainforests' influence on the world's climate.

Monsoon Forest
Bali and the eastern half of Java fall under the seasonal influence of the monsoons, with daily downpours of heavy rain falling from late October until April. For the rest of the year the climate is essentially dry, more so than elsewhere in Java or in Sumatra, Borneo or Malaysia, and it is this seasonal lack of water that has a profound effect on the climate.
With annual rainfalls less than 80

PEACE AND QUIET

inches (2,000mm) and with such seasonal variation, true rainforest trees cannot survive. Teak and other drought-tolerant species do thrive, however, and give rise to a special type of forest known as monsoon forest. During the dry season, some of the trees lose their leaves and the forest may look dry and lifeless, but with the coming of the monsoons, the foliage becomes lush again, flowers burst into bloom and insect populations flourish.

Search among the foliage and fallen leaf litter and you will soon find an extraordinary variety of insects. Cicadas and bush crickets sing noisily but are often difficult to locate; many of the other creatures are easier to find. Some, like the ants, are small and seemingly everywhere you look, while metallic rhinoceros beetles and giant atlas moths are less numerous but immediately noticeable because of their size. Birdwatching may prove a little

An atlas beetle

more challenging than searching for invertebrates. Although birds of prey, such as crested hawk eagles, may circle overhead, and woodpeckers and drongos feed or perch on exposed branches, other species are more elusive. Forest floor species, such as pittas, thrushes and junglefowl, feed unobtrusively. Early morning walks along quiet trails and paths, preferably on your own or in the company of a few like-minded people, will produce the best sightings. Listen for feeding birds rustling the leaves and creep quietly towards the source of the sound – and you may be lucky. Outside the breeding season, many of the forest's smaller birds roam around in mixed feeding flocks aften comprising 20 species or more. Do not be disheartened by an initial apparent lack of birds: at any moment a mixed flock might pass overhead providing the bewildering, if albeit brief, spectacle of several hundred birds.

Blue-tailed banded pitta

Paddy Fields

Rice is probably the single most important crop to be grown on Bali as well as on much of Java. This tropical grass thrives in wetland conditions, and vast areas of paddy cover much of the lowlands, creating a mosaic of flooded fields. Every suitable piece of land is used for rice, as well as some not so suitable areas. Not even hillsides escape the steady march of cultivation: terraces, watered by cunning networks of canals and aqueducts, are a testament to man's ingenuity and a rotation of crop planting allows harvesting throughout the year. Although the natural vegetation of the region has necessarily been cleared to make way for the rice fields, some wildlife still manages to survive. Frog, insect, and, in some areas, fish populations are high and support large numbers of birds, such as adjutant storks, kingfishers, herons, egrets and birds of prey. From October until March large flocks of migrant waders occur although the species found in them – and their distribution – are rather unpredictable.

Around the Coast

Away from centres of population, visitors to Bali and Java can find beautiful sandy beaches fringed with palms, rocky headlands, coral reefs and estuaries and mangrove swamps, all bathed by the warm waters of the Indian Ocean to the south and the Javan Sea to the north. These are rich in marine life and support thriving populations of both oceanic and coastal birds. Coral reefs provide a truly astonishing spectacle. Often just a short distance below the surface, colourful corals, anemones and sea fans harbour a myriad of colourful fish, smaller species in shoals and larger fish patrolling territories. Scuba diving is the ultimate way to explore the reef but a simple snorkel and mask is all you really need to enter this world. During periods of onshore winds, particularly along the rougher southern shores, and on ferry crossings, a variety of seabirds may be seen. Sooty and bridled terns are truly oceanic species while crested terns are more frequently encountered closer to shore. Keen-eyed observers may spot Swinhoe's storm petrels, their dark plumage and forked tails aiding identification, or a Christmas Island frigatebird wheeling overhead with its immense wingspan. Where shoals of fish have attracted seabirds, keep a lookout for dolphins and whales which may also be lured by the marine bonanza.

Were it not for disturbance and the regrettable Indonesian liking for their meat and eggs, turtles would nest on sandy beaches all around Bali and Java. Loggerhead, Pacific, Ridley, leatherback, green and hawksbill turtles are now restricted to remote or protected areas such as the Nusa Barung Island reserve off southeast Java, Sukomade Beach in southwest Java or Serangan Island off south Bali. Females, which come ashore at

PEACE AND QUIET

night to lay their leathery eggs in pits excavated in the sand, are cumbersome and vulnerable on land, making them easy prey to local plunderers. Such is the scale and efficiency of the depredations that populations of turtles are under serious threat. Visitors who want to show their disquiet should refuse turtle meat or eggs as well as artefacts made from turtle-shell.

Mangroves

Mangrove swamps grow throughout Indonesia wherever silt-laden rivers meet the sea and form suitable estuaries. Good examples can be seen around Gilimanuk in northwest Bali, near Denpasar and at Baluran in northeast Java. The key element in the formation of mangrove swamps is silt: it must be nutrient-rich and there must be plenty of it. Several species of mangrove can be found in the region but all share a tolerance of saltwater and an ability to grow in choking silt. Their characteristic tangled network of roots encourages the deposition of silt and so the swamps help create new dry land. Mangrove swamps are incredible places for naturalists. Armies of fiddler crabs, hermit crabs, ghost crabs and amphibious crabs scurry across the surface of the mud at low tide, accompanied by mudskippers, curious fish which spend much of their lives out of water. Some crabs fall victim to crab-eating macaques while several species of kingfishers, egrets and herons also take a toll. Both macaques and herons,

as well as human visitors, have to keep a wary eye open, as the tide rises, for saltwater crocodiles.

Komodo Dragons

Pulau Komodo and neighbouring islands, now a national park, are home to one of the world's most extraordinary creatures, the Komodo dragon. This relict from the age of the dinosaurs thrives on the islands in the absence of competing carnivores and is becoming a major tourist attraction. To reach Komodo still requires time, effort and money. The island can be reached by island-hopping using ferries and buses which will take several days. Visitors can sometimes join organised tours from Denpasar. Permits to enter the national park should be bought in advance from a Forestry Authority (PPA) office. Although a dragon in name only, and in reality a species of monitor lizard, the Komodo dragon is no less impressive for it. Adults can reach a length of 6½ feet (2m) and weigh up to 110lbs (50kg) and will kill prey as large as wild buffalo, wild pigs, deer and goats. Despite their ability to tackle live animals, the dragons are lured by the smell of carrion, using a keen sense of smell; visitors, who must always be accompanied by guides from Loho Liang, often use dead goats as a bait. However, if you are offended by the idea of sacrificing a goat, Komodo dragons can usually also be found simply by following their tracks.

FOOD AND DRINK

Indonesian Cuisine

Rice is the staple diet of most people throughout Indonesia. Coconut-milk, hot chillies and spices are common ingredients. Traditional dishes are *gado-gado* (cold vegetable salad with peanut sauce), *soto* (a spicy broth), *saté* (char-grilled meat, poultry or fish) and *nasi goreng* (fried rice usually with vegetables or egg).

Seafood is readily available in Indonesia and very good. Tropical fruits are also abundant.

Beverages are fruit-juices, coffee or tea, rice-wine and excellent beer manufactured under patent to Heineken. There are many Chinese as well as Western-style restaurants in Jakarta and in the tourist towns on Bali. For recommendations see **Jakarta** pages 30–4 and under individual entries in **What to See in Bali**.

Balinese Food

Balinese food is blander than elsewhere in Indonesia as cooks use fewer spices and chillies. The major difference, however, is that pork, which is anathema to Muslims, is eaten on Bali. Roast suckling pig, or *babi guling* is the island's traditional dish. Duck steamed in a banana leaf, *betutu bebek* is another. The Balinese are also unique in eating turtle, imported from the Moluccas or raised on Serangan Island (see page 67). *Lawar* – raw meat mixed with blood – is also popular. Prepared at home, it is on sale – and eaten – within the hour because of the climate. Country people eat frogs,

Saté *(char-grilled meat or fish) and peanut dip is a hot and spicy Indonesian dish*

worms, snakes, paddy eels, flying-foxes, lizards and dragonflies. Children trap the latter on a wispy pole with a sticky end.

If nothing else, any restaurant patronised by tourists will have *nasi goreng, gado gado* and *saté* on the menu. Common side dishes are cucumber pickle and prawn crackers or *krupek* – delicious when fresh. Fresh seafood is hard to find. It is in fact difficult to find genuine Balinese food. Your best chance is at a traditional dance and buffet night at one of the international hotels. The **Bali Oberoi** in Legian does an excellent Indonesian buffet with *babi guling*. The genial Balinese chef at **La Taverna Hotel** in

FOOD AND DRINK

Sanur cooks island specialities such as *betutu bebek*. As in Jakarta, although they are not so good, *warung* or street stalls are recommended. Night markets have a mix of Chinese as well as Indonesian food. Common items are *mi-goreng* (fried wheatflour noodles) and *chapchaai* (an elaborate version of chop-suey). One stall will always specialise in *soto nasi goreng* and *nasi campur* (steamed or boiled rice with vegetables, meat or fish). Instead of soya sauce favoured by the Chinese, you get a small dish of *sambal*, a fiery dip made from chillies, dried shrimp paste and lime-juice.

Balinese love snacks. Everywhere are people selling tiny packets of food, rice-cakes and crunchy biscuits. Most things are a mystery: you need an Indonesian-speaking companion to explain. The Central Market in Denpasar is filled with snack-stalls. Try *onde-onde*, delicious sesame-seed studded balls of blue rice with bean paste and palm sugar fillings. You can eat your fill for around £1.50.

Apart from on ceremonial occasions, the Balinese are modest eaters. The two or three daily meals revolve around boiled white rice, with small portions of lightly spiced meat or poultry, vegetables, peanuts and cucumber. There are no set meal times; people eat when they are hungry. Food is cooked in the early morning and left in covered pots on the kitchen table. Eating is normally not communal as members of the family come in at odd times

to serve themselves.

Feasts are different. Preparing food for all the relatives at a wedding, or a funeral, may take all night until morning. The men gather to prepare *lawar*, and the suckling pigs. When preparations are complete, portions are divided on banana-leaf 'plates' for offering to the gods before everyone eats. The gods are fed every day. If you are up early, you will see young girls quietly leaving tiny trays outside the shrines. Those placed on the ground are devoured by dogs. The Balinese eat with their right hand, taking a lump of rice, dipping it in *sambal* and inserting in the mouth with the thumb. Water is commonly drunk with a meal.

Balinese Beverages

Tea *(teh)* is popular. Fragrant, like Chinese tea, it is drunk hot, or cold, with sugar *(manis)* or without *(pahit)*. Coffee is rarely well made. Strong, it has lots of grounds floating. Black coffee is *kopi Bali* and white, *kopi susu.* **Made's Warung** in Kuta (see page 56), knows how to prepare good espresso-style coffee. Alcoholic beverages include *brem* (rice-wine), *arak* (distilled rice brandy), and *tuak* (sweet palm-beer). Old *brem* (*brem tua*) is more expensive; drinking too much may give you a headache. Local bottled 'Ankor' and 'Bintang' are pleasant, light lager with a lower alcohol content than Western beer. Outside tourist-resorts it is hard to find cold beer. Beer *pakai es* (with ice) is proffered, but best refused. Familiar

Western soft drinks are readily available; but try the Balinese bottled drinks like *Temulawak,* a spicy, fizzy concoction. Bottled mineral water is also available. Fresh fruit-juices are very popular thirst-quenchers in Bali; they are also sold in cartons. *Jeruk* is the general name for citrus fruit; *air jeruk* (orange juice) and *air jeruk nipis* (lemon juice) may be sold hot, or cold. Cool juices are made from pineapple, mango, apple, papaya, passionfruit, banana, litchi and other fruits. There is a drinks stand outside every market. Some of the beverages are exotic concoctions like *es kopyor,* made from rose syrup, ice and tender lumps of coconut jelly. Equally delicious is *es campur,* a blend of jelly, fruit and shaved ice. Beware of anything made with ice unfortunately.

A treat for the eye and the appetite: exotic Balinese fruits

Fruits

Bali grows an abundance of tropical fruits; familiar types such as bananas, plus exotic species like *salak,* a heart-shaped apple covered in snake-like skin. You should try the following – all are sold in Denpasar, depending on the season.

Blimbing*:* starfruit or carambola – cool, crisp, yellow fruit which resembles a star when cut.

Durian*:* huge, greenish-yellow spiky fruit greatly revered by locals. Smells like rotten cheese; tastes like creamy banana custard.

Mangosteen*:* about the size of a billiard ball, with smooth purple skin which stains your fingers. The green segments on top are said to resemble, exactly, the luscious white lobes within. Balinese bet on how many lobes there will be, from one to eight. Slightly tart taste of litchi and passionfruit.

Nangcur: or jackfruit – the largest fruit in the world – may weigh up to 44lbs (20kilos). Knobbly yellowish-green skin. Bright yellow, slightly rubbery segments.

Passionfruit: if you think you know passionfruit, wait until you see the huge, yellow-skinned passionfruit grown around Kintamani. Milder tasting than familiar purple varieties.

Rambutan: round, hairy greenish-red fruit. Sweet, soft, translucent flesh, with a taste similar to litchi.

Salak: or snake-fruit. Peculiar apple-textured fruit. Grows around Rendang, and slopes of Gunung Agung.

Zuzat: or custard apple. Warty blackish-green skin covering slightly tart segments. Best eaten when slightly soft.

SHOPPING

Bali is a treasure-house of unusual arts and crafts objects. Everyone on the island seems to be creative. In some villages entire families are painters and sculptors. Their talents are natural and they have loads of time. Except for weavers, artists are generally male. Previously they used to paint and sculpt for enjoyment; the tourist market now provides an income. Unfortunately tourism, or what Balinese perceive to be foreign taste, is also flooding the shops with trash, and cheap souvenirs are thrust at visitors to every tourist attraction.

For anyone interested in acquiring something of integrity and quality, here is a brief guide to Balinese arts and crafts.

Painting

With stone-carving, painting is the most exuberant talent exhibited in Bali. Isolated from outside influence, island artists originally portrayed narrative themes from Hindu mythology; bizarre creatures frolicked and fought against a Rousseau-type backdrop of jungle foliage, covering every inch of space. This infinite artistic energy was channelled into three types of painting: large, decorative works for palaces and temples; temple scrolls; and astrological calendars. Paintings were executed in narrative panels with the characters shown in profile. Vivid examples of this style can be seen in Klungkung (see page 54).

Painting changed when Western artists Walter Spies and Rudolf Bonnet came to Bali in the 1930s. Influenced by their work, local artists switched to realism. Scenes of everyday rural life, temple processions and dances became the subject of single pictures. The new trend caught on in the lively arts centres of Mas-Ubud. Political upheaval in the mid-1960s threw many artists into despair but spirits revived with encouragement from Dutch artist Arie Smit. He taught European methods, leaving the choice of subject and composition to the native artists. This new genre of painting known as the 'young artists' developed in Penestan, near Ubud. Busy and colourful is one description of the 'young artist' school.

In truth it is hard to find a contemporary work that pleases enough to buy. Much of the market is happy to have a 'Bali original' without caring about its merits.Galleries are chock-a-block with gharish paintings, one like the next. If you wish to buy, be guided by early works in museums such as the Puri Lukisan in Ubud (see page 72).

Woodcarving

Balinese are some of the most skilled woodcarvers in Indonesia. Spectacular carvings are everywhere you look: doors, temple struts, free-standing statues and domestic objects. Wood-carving was originally done only for royalty and high-caste families. Changes from traditional styles began in the 1930s. At first they were subtle – the elongated female torso is an example – but new art-forms emerged. Encouraged by commercial interest, woodcarvers scaled down their sculpture. Small figures and scenes from ordinary life replaced creatures from the ancient epics. Realism became a theme in wood-carving communities in Mas-Ubud. Some celebrated sculptors such as Ida Bagus Tilem of Mas continue to carve abstract representations of the human figure, but influenced by tourist taste; others have turned to pop art. Frogs, birds, pigs and familiar objects are depicted with humour and occasional vulgarity. Carved wooden phalluses are a sign of the times. And, strangely for an island where cats are rare, feline ornaments are hugely popular. Some workshops in Mas specialise in cats – highly

An example of the artistry of Bali's woodcarvers, this stunning mask was produced in Mas

exaggerated, decoratively painted cats – hundreds of them.

Ebony from Sulawesi is the usual choice for classic pieces. It has a fine grain and, when polished, a rich, dark lustre. Some dealers try to cheat by selling local woods like *sawo* and *bentawas.* They are similar, but ebony is heavier. It is also more expensive – about triple the price. Like all master artists, the Balinese produce their share of fakes usually temple artefacts which they call antiques. Attractive, inexpensive carvings feature popular fruits so genuine you could bite them.

SHOPPING

Transitory Art-forms

The purest and oldest form of Balinese art is *lamaks*. You can never be tricked into buying an antique, as a *lamak* only lasts a day. They are woven from palm leaf and bamboo folded in hundreds of different ways. You will see them hanging in the temple during a festival. Other perishable art-forms include the spectacular temple offerings made by women, and the giant sarcophagi which go up in smoke on a funeral pyre.

Silverwork

Filigreework made by silversmiths in Celuk and Gianyar has ancient Indian origins: you see similar designs in downtown Delhi. Spinning methods remain primitive and apprentices begin young; some are expert by their teens. Hawkers flogging silver jewellery are a nuisance in Kuta-Legian. Telling them you only like gold is a deterrent. Silver ceremonial daggers, or *kris,* are an interesting proposition. A man's economic status was judged by the richly embellished handle, or sheath. Making a *kris* is time-consuming and they are therefore expensive. Old ones are rarely offered for sale, being family heirlooms.

Weaving

Weaving remains part of a traditional Balinese woman's upbringing. Fabrics vary from simple homespun cotton *sarong* to rich *songket* cloth worked with gold and silver thread. The districts of Klungkung and Karasem are renowned for silk brocade. Bali is also one of the few remaining centres making *ikat*, a time-consuming process, involving dyeing each thread prior to weaving a pattern. As with purchasing a fine Persian carpet, a little knowledge of *ikat* is useful if you intend to buy fabric. (See **Tenganan**, page 70). *Sarong* vary in price. They may cost ten times more than normal at a temple festival.

Other Crafts

Hand-painted kites, wind-chimes, shell objects and basketware are other eye-catching crafts. What is inexpensive, however, may not be a bargain. For instance, a cheap raffish hat will have been woven with green straw and will therefore quickly lose its shape.
Craftsmen also make shadow puppets (*wayang kulit*) and delicate, lace-like fans from buffalo hide. A list of all Bali's hand-crafted goods is endless; it is essential to buy carefully and bargain for anything you fancy.

Bargaining

Most Western travellers feel uncomfortable bargaining, but it is traditional in Asia and should be regarded as a challenge. It can be good fun as well as saving you money. Try to slash at least 25 per cent off the first price.
If you do not want to haggle, shop at Sanagraha Kriya Asta, the government handicraft centre on the Tohpati Road, north of Sanur (see **Denpasar** page 48).

For information on shopping in Jakarta, see pages 34–36.

ACCOMMODATION

Bali has a variety of accommodation ranging from basic *losmen* to de luxe hotels. *Losmen* are small cheap inns which often follow the pattern of a Balinese home. This means that, although you have your own bedroom, you spend much of the time communally in the inner garden with the family and other guests – a great way to meet people and experience something of Balinese everyday life. There is even more sharing in homestays, which are licensed private homes. Tariffs for accommodation are quoted in Indonesian *rupiah* or US dollars. A 15.5 per cent tax and service charge is billed by large hotels. *Losmen* and homestays charge a flat rate, often negotiable, and expect cash. At time of writing, the amount you can expect to

The massive 62-acre (13-hectare) complex of the Jakarta Hilton Hotel

pay per night for accommodation, and what you will get for your money, is as follows:

Cheap: Rp10,000-20,000. Basic, usually clean. Often shared facilities, WC.

Moderate: Rp30,000-60,000. A clean, usually comfortable room with private bathroom. Excellent value in some cases with traditional Balinese décor and superb views. Likely to have a restaurant/bar and offer most hotel facilities on a modest scale.

Expensive: upwards of Rp80,000-100,000. Clean, and with professional management. All facilities including swimming pool and shop. Credit cards accepted. Will be used by package tours.

Very expensive: prices are quoted in dollars only, upwards of $150. International standard hotel which would be double the price in Europe.

ACCOMMODATION/CULTURE AND ENTERTAINMENT

Choosing Where to Stay

Where possible book in advance. If you do not hold a reservation, check in at the hotel desk at Denpasar Airport. Hotel representatives wait outside. Choose a familiar name on your first night, then change to somewhere cheaper. *Losmen* are two a penny in places like Kuta-Legian. Visit half a dozen, or more, until you find one you like. Ask to see the room and bathroom. This is acceptable practice throughout Indonesia. Most are safe, but do not flaunt your valuables; use safe-deposit facilities for spare cash, etc. Some homestays treat you like a member of the family.

In busy tourist periods, bookings are essential in Sanur and Ubud. Ubud has the best moderately priced accommodation in Bali: standards are often extremely high for a modest Rp35,000. For recommended accommodation in **Jakarta**, see pages 28–29.

All hotels recommended in this book were personally checked, but no responsibility is taken for subsequent changes.

CULTURE AND ENTERTAINMENT

The performing arts on Bali are very much interlinked, with dances being dramatic enactments of mythological events to musical accompaniment. Most visitors will attend a performance of some kind during their stay; despite their strangeness to Western ears and eyes, Balinese music and dance can be greatly enjoyed.

Balinese music is best represented by the ancient form of gamelan

Music

There are many musical forms in Indonesia, but the most widespread and highly developed is the *gamelan*. So central is it that the entire orchestra is known as a *gamelan*. It reaches perfection on the islands of Bali and Java. The rippling chords of the *gamelan* are to Bali what the bagpipes are to Scotland, and you will hear it everywhere. Almost entirely percussion, a full *gamelan* orchestra may consist of as many as 80 individual instruments, divided into two separate, but complementary sets. Each is tuned to a different scale. Indeed, no two *gamelans* are tuned identically. These sets of drums, xylophones,

CULTURE AND ENTERTAINMENT

Peliatan, Ubud, every Sunday 19.30–21.00 hrs; Puri Saren, Ubud, every Monday 19.30–21.00 hrs; Br. Tegal, Kuta, every Tuesday, Saturday, 20.00 hrs.

Shadow Puppet Show: Mars Hotel, Sanur (tel: 88236), every Tuesday, Thursday, Sunday, 18.00–21.00 hrs; Oka Kartini, Tebesaya Peliatan, every Sunday, 20.00–21.00 hrs.

Tek Tekan Dance: Puri Anyar, Kerambitan, Tabanan. Times on request.

Mahabharata: Br. Teges, Peliatan, every Tuesday, 18.30–20.00 hrs.

Frog Dance: Penjor Restaurant, Sanur, every Sunday, 19.00 hrs.

Parwa Ramayana: Hotel Menara, Ubud, every Tuesday, Wednesday, 20.00 hrs.

Hotel Entertainment

Many of the hotels in the main resorts of Kuta, Sanur and Nusa Dua lay on entertainment of various sorts. Below is a guide to some of the treats on offer.

Music

Hotel Bali Beach, Sanur: 'Bali Hai Supper Club' – international, nightly 21.30 hrs Monday to Saturday.

Nusa Dua Beach Hotel, near the car park-poolside, *Angklung-gamelan*, Wednesday from 19.30 hrs. Frog dance Tuesday, 20.00 hrs.

Hotel Melia Bali Sol, Nusa Dua: Music Room – *Laserdisc Karaoke*, nightly 21.00–midnight. Piano bar nightly from 20.00 hrs.

Pertamina Cottages, Kuta Beach: poolside music with barbecue from 19.00 hrs Saturday. Country music Monday from 19.00 hrs.

Sahid Bali Seaside Hotel, pool terrace – band and international buffet, Sunday from 19.30 hrs. Oriental buffet, Wednesday from 19.30 hrs.

The kechak dance is performed to a vocal accompaniment intended to suggest the chattering of monkeys

Traditional Dance

Hotel Bali Beach, Sanur: *Legong*, Monday from 19.00 hrs.
Hotel Bali Hyatt, Sanur: *Pasar Malam* (Night Market) with Frog Dance, Monday from 19.30 hrs. *Ramayana* Ballet with *rijstaffel*, Wednesday from 19.30 hrs.
Hotel Sanur Beach, Sanur: *Legong* dance/buffet, Monday from 19.30 hrs. *Ramayana* Ballet/buffet, Tuesday from 19.30 hrs.
Nusa Dua Beach Hotel: *Ramayana*/buffet, Monday from 19.00 hrs. *Legong*/buffet, Friday from 19.00 hrs.
Hotel Melia Bali Sol, Nusa Dua: *Legong*/international buffet, Tuesday from 19.30 hrs. *Kechak*/barbecue, Saturday from 19.30 hrs. Puppet Theatre, Wednesday from 18.30 hrs.
Hotel Putra Bali, Nusa Dua: *Ramayana* Ballet/seafood buffet, Monday from 19.30 hrs. *Legong*/suckling pig, Thursday from 19.30 hrs. *Barong*, Friday from 19.30 hrs. Frog Dance/ barbecue, Saturday from 20.00 hrs.
Pertamina Cottages, Kuta Beach: *Legong*, Sunday from 19.00 hrs. Frog Dance, Wednesday from 19.00 hrs. *Ramayana* Ballet, Friday from 19.00 hrs.
Sahid Bali Seaside Hotel: *Legong*/barbecue, Monday from 19.30 hrs. *Ramayana* Ballet, Thursday from 19.30 hrs.
Bali Oberoi Hotel, Legian Beach: *Angklung-gamelan*, Monday; *Legong*/seafood, Tuesday; *Pasar Malam* and *Ramayana* Ballet, Thursday; *Rajapala*/barbecue, Saturday; *Kechak*/rijstaffel, Saturday; Indonesian poolside buffet/ cultural show, Sunday. Usual start-time 18.30 hrs.

WEATHER AND WHEN TO GO

Indonesia as a whole has an equatorial climate tempered by trade winds. There are two seasons: dry (between April and October) and wet (from November to March). The

*The tropical rains descend on
Taman Mini bird park, Jakarta*

average annual temperature is
27°C (80°F) in the lowlands and
about 22°C (71°F) in elevated
areas.
Bali has a generally agreeable
climate except before the
monsoon season when it is
unpleasantly hot with humidity
of 95 per cent. Tropical
downpours alternate with
sunshine during the wet season
from October to March
(particularly bad in late
January/early February). Sunny
days with moderate humidity
occur from May to September,
the best time to visit Bali.
Average coastal temperature
varies from about 28°C (82°F)
from May to July to about 30°C
(86°F) in March and October.
Within 1½ hours' drive of the
coast, highland temperatures
are cooler – 16-28°C (61-82°F).
Prospective visitors from the
northern hemisphere should
note that Bali is very popular
with Australians, and Christmas
is a particularly busy time. The
low season is January to May,
and this is the time to go to
avoid the crowds.

HOW TO BE A LOCAL

You are never going to be
mistaken for a native on Bali,
but some knowledge of social
customs and etiquette may
prevent the visitor from
appearing totally insensitive to
Balinese ways.

Everyday Life
Every stage of Balinese life is
marked by ceremony of one
sort or another.

Birth
Balinese adore children and
have plenty to prove it. At the
third month of pregnancy,
offerings are made to ensure
the well-being of the foetus.
After the birth, the placenta is
buried with suitable offerings
and 12 days later the mother is
purified in a cleansing
ceremony. When the baby is
210 days old, its feet are

HOW TO BE A LOCAL

allowed to touch the ground for the first time, and it is officially welcomed into the family. Twins of different sexes are a catastrophe as they are believed to have committed incest in the womb. Costly ceremonies must be held to purify everyone in the household.

There are only four first names on Bali. Children are named according to the order in which they are born. The first child is Wayan, second Made, third Nyoman and fourth, Ketut. Fifth to eighth are the same again. First-born boys are also known as Gede; Putu is the name of the first-born girl.

Only when a Balinese baby is 210 days old do its feet touch the ground for the first time

Marriage
Balinese marry young. Marriages are not arranged, but they must relate to caste (see next page). Elopement is cheap and appeals to the Balinese fun-loving nature. When the lovers emerge from hiding, their marriage is officially recognised by the families.

Death and Cremation see page 14.

Sexual Roles
Balinese have few social hang-ups. The sexes mix freely but roles are strictly spelled out. Women work much harder. As well as being responsible for running the household, they also buy and sell: 90 per cent of market traders are women. Women also make daily offerings to the temple. What do the men do? They till the fields and plant the rice and while the rice is growing, they do very little. They spend hours talking to friends and preening their fighting cocks. Artistic skills are almost exclusively male-oriented, although both sexes perform traditional dances.

The Home
A traditional Balinese house is surrounded by a high wall enclosing a garden with specific buildings for cooking, ablutions and sleeping. The living room is an open pavilion shaded by a tree, because in the hot climate people tend to live outdoors. Only Western-type homes in Denpasar-Sanur have air conditioning. The actual gateway into the house is staggered to prevent evil spirits simply scooting in. Animals –

dogs, the huge sway-backed pigs and chickens – share the domestic compound.

Village Life

Each adult male joins the village committee – the *banjar* – when he marries. The *banjar* is responsible for decision making: the date of the next cockfight, the hour for *gamelan* practice, etc. Meetings are held on a dirt square shaded by a huge banyan tree. At the main intersection in the village, this is the centre of community life. The village market is also found here, but the *banjar* is an all-male club.

Caste

Like India, Bali has a caste system. Though less strict, it dictates social etiquette, in particular how Balinese address each other. The working class, or village peasants (*Sudras*) constitute the lowest rank. Nobility is divided into three castes. *Brahmans* are the highest caste (only a Brahman may become a high priest); men may have the title *Ida Bagus*. The *Satrias* have the honorific titles of *Anak Agung*, *Dewa* and *Cokorda*, and the *Vaishyas* are former rulers of local principalities with the title *I Gusti*. The Bali Aga are casteless, but there are no untouchables.

Etiquette demands one must be addressed according to one's caste. Hence a Sudra will address a Brahman in a higher form of Balinese. The person of a higher caste will respond using 'village Balinese'. There is also a 'middle Balinese', used when caste is not involved. As

well as speaking Balinese, people also speak *Bahasa Indonesia*. Adept linguists, many young people – specifically those associated with tourism – speak English, German or Italian. Bright sparks are also learning Japanese.

Social Etiquette

Social etiquette plays a major part in Balinese life. Respecting traditional ways is appreciated: breaking religious and social taboos may cause offence. It is rude to point with your foot at someone. For those who do not know each other well, touching the other's head is impolite. You are welcome to watch most ritual ceremonies provided you are properly dressed. The unfortunate Balinese are accustomed to scantily dressed Australians, but do wear something decent to visit the temples. Do not stand where the priest will appear smaller than you are and never walk in front of people who are praying. Women may not enter a temple during their menstruation. Notices outside temples advise women of this requirement. A temple sash is compulsory. It is a good plan to take a sash, or long cotton or silk scarf from home, or buy a *sarong* locally. The alternative is to pay for a sash outside each temple.

Dogs

Precisely who owns the obnoxious local dogs is uncertain. No one seems to take any care or responsibility for dogs in Bali. Irritable, dirty and diseased, they go a long way to spoiling an island holiday. Even if you like dogs, you will find

Balinese dogs *ghastly*. Sleep is often ruined by packs of dogs barking at each other across the rice fields. When they howl, the Balinese say they are talking to their ancestors, and do nothing to stop them. Throwing stones, the room vase or your suitcase at them is bad form. *Cicings* (a strong Balinese word for disgusting curs) are especially vile around Mas-Ubud, Semawang and on Nusa Penida. It is advisable to take ear-plugs.

PERSONAL PRIORITIES

The Female Traveller
Older, experienced women travellers will probably enjoy a holiday in Jakarta and Bali. But as a lone woman, particularly if using public transport, you should be especially alert. Only experience can avoid some situations. If driving in Bali, a little mechanical knowledge is useful.

Younger women should not become over-friendly with strangers. Play it cool, dress discreetly, and act in a manner that warrants respect. Young female tourists have a bad reputation in Kuta-Sanur due to the behaviour of some Australian girls. An invitation from one Balinese 'beach-boy' is likely to involve his friends. Use a reliable taxi service to commute after dark. It is advisable to spend more, rather than less, on accommodation. Cheap *losmen* attract 'camp-followers'. A little Indonesian may be useful: *saya senag sendiri* means 'I like to be alone', *pergi* means 'go away!'.

Babies
Up-market hotels and *losmen* can arrange baby-sitters, although taking a young baby is tough on mother and infant unless you stay in a good, air-conditioned hotel. Nappies are sold in Jakarta department stores and also in Kuta and Sanur. If a child is old enough, a backpack carrier is invaluable.

Venereal Diseases
Jakarta has its share of common venereal diseases, but nothing like Manila, or Bangkok. So far it is missing the AIDS epidemic – isolated cases in Bali have been foreigners. If you think you have caught something, have a lab-test done at the nearest public hospital.

What to Wear
Lightweight cotton trousers and shirts, skirts and blouses, and sportswear are best in the tropical climate of Bali and Jakarta. Dress is very casual on Bali where shorts are acceptable anywhere except temples (see page 103). You will need a warm sweater and waterproof jacket for the mountains and good shoes if you plan climbing the volcanoes. Jakarta is more 'dressed up'. Casual wear is okay in moderately priced hotels, but guests dress at night in better establishments. Waterproof clothing and an umbrella are essential during the monsoon season.

CHILDREN

Some areas in Indonesia are unsuited to family holidays, but Bali and Jakarta are recommended. Balinese love children and children find Bali a fantasy-land. For short stays, Jakarta has recreational parks, zoos and other entertainment. Pulau Seribu islands are ideal for an outdoor family holiday. The many colourful dance and puppet theatre performances on Bali make wonderful entertainment for children of all ages. And of course the beaches will keep a small child happy all day. However, a word of warning: do not leave your child playing with Balinese children; splashing in the shallows, they can attract in a toddler who cannot swim.

TIGHT BUDGET

You can exist for as little as Rp 15,000 (£10.50 or $16) a day (accommodation/meals/drinks) in Bali. This rises to Rp 40,000 (£28 or $42) in Jakarta. For a mere Rp 500 (35p or ¢50) you have a choice of: six fried bananas from a street stall; four oranges; a packet (12) of local cigarettes; an airmail stamp for Europe; the English language newspaper; or a shoe-shine (with change).

If your cash is limited, you should perhaps think of visiting Bali in the low season (March to May) when hotel tariffs are reduced – sometimes by as much as 50 per cent. In any case, a homestay or *losmen* provides cheap, and often quite comfortable, lodging. Jakarta is expensive, but some cheaper rooms are available if you are there in time to snap them up. See page 29 for some recommended cheaper hotels.

Market restaurants are a cost-cutting option for meals

Eating can be inexpensive and tasty if you patronise the street stalls that abound in the towns. *Warung* are night foodstalls, open from twilight to about midnight and serving delicious authentic Indonesian food. Remember, however, that *Ramadan* in Muslim Jakarta is not a good time for finding cheap food – expensive Chinese restaurants may be the only places serving meals.

SPECIAL EVENTS

Islamic holidays dominate the religious calendar in Indonesia where 87 per cent of people are Muslims, but every ethnic and religious group – Chinese, Balinese, Christian – celebrates its own festivals. The result is a confusing calendar of events where virtually every day is a nominal holiday.

SPECIAL EVENTS

Jakarta

The Javanese calendar is based on the lunar year (354 days), and varies by about 11 days from year to year. Some of the major Islamic holidays may cause travel inconvenience. *Ramadan* – the fast month – is best avoided in any Muslim country, and during the two-day festival of *Hari Raya* as many as 80 million Javanese are using public transport.

Lebaran, or *Hari Raya*, occurs on the first day of the tenth month after *Ramadan*. Mass prayers are said in mosques and people wear new clothes and exchange presents and food. Like Christmas, St Valentine's Day and New Year rolled in one, *lebaran* celebrations may last a week. Everything is closed on the first two days of *lebaran* in Jakarta. The other major Islamic holiday, *Grebeg Besar*, occurs on the 10th day of the eleventh lunar month, after the annual pilgrimage to Mecca. It is marked by sacrifices when your hotel may slaughter a sheep or goat in the garden for its staff. Meat is distributed to the needy.

Bali

Nyepi is the Balinese 'New Year'. It falls on the spring equinox, and on this day no fire may be lit, no activity carried on and all transport stops. Huge offerings are laid on the crossroads to appease the evil spirits. That night everyone goes out banging gongs, blowing whistles and making as much noise as possible to scare off malevolent spirits for another year.

Temples play an important part in Balinese life, and special occasions are marked with elaborate offerings

Galungan is held annually when the supreme god, Ida Sanghyang Widhi Wasa is believed to descend to earth. Sacrifices of pigs, chickens and ducks are made in his honour. Long, decorated bamboo poles, (*penjors*) are erected outside each house in gratitude for prosperity. During the 10-day festival, *barongs* are taken out of the temples and prance from village to village. On the final day, known as *Kuningan*, when Sanghyang Widhi and other deities depart, offerings are made in their honour. Notable temples where *Galungan* and *Kuningan* ceremonies can be seen are at:

Mengwi, Ulu Watu, Tanah Lot, Goa Lawah and Serangan.

Other Holidays
Kartini Day, 21 April, is a national holiday, commemorating the birthday of Ajeng Kartini (1870-1903), a pioneer in the struggle for the emancipation of Indonesian women. Women wear their national dress on this day.
Proklomasi Kemerdekaan (Independence Day), 17 August, is Indonesian National Independence Day, marked by different celebrations throughout the archipelago.
Armed Forces Day, 5 October, is a public holiday when military parades and army, navy and airforce demonstrations are staged in Jakarta.

SPORT
Popular Pastimes
Cockfighting
Cockfights are illegal, but Balinese take no notice. Banning horse racing would amount to the same thing in England or America. Until it fights, a cock leads a life of luxury. It is fed on a special diet, its feathers are preened and its muscles massaged by an adorning owner. A pet as well as a potential means of income, the bird is carried lovingly wherever its owner goes. You will see men sitting under the village banyan-tree with their cocks. They are taken to *warung* and to village meetings. When the owner goes to the fields, his bird is placed in a bell-shaped bamboo cage, which is stood with others on the roadside for company. With the melodious *gamelan*, the sound of crowing cocks is unmistakable Bali. Cockfights are usually held on the occasion of a temple festival. A group of men – women are not present – gathers outside the gate. Handlers hold the birds aloft for appraisal. Boys rush about collecting bets; sometimes a village may wager a million *rupiah* on a popular fighting cock. When everything is ready, the fight is blessed. The cock's feathers are ruffled and his tail is pulled, but being naturally aggressive the two birds attack. Each rakes the other with razor-spurs tied on to its legs. Dust and features fly. Most cockfights are over within 15 seconds with one bird lying mortally injured. Occasionally it

is revived by a 'kiss of life' and the audience becomes hysterical as the fight goes on.

Kite-Flying

Balinese adore kite-flying. Graceful kites are believed to please Rare Angon, the shepherd god. Kites are huge, often 26 feet (8m) long, needing a dozen men to launch. The strange 'whoop-whoop-whoop' noise made by the kites is familiar over Sanur and Serangan, where they actually pose a threat to aircraft. *Garuda* and other bird-shaped kites are attractive souvenirs. Villages compete against each other, and the pastime has even become international here now. The biennial international kite-flying contest is held between Sanur and Tohpati in July, August or September.

Bullock-racing

Bullock-races are held after the harvest season in Singaraja and Negara. (See pages 59 and 67). The programme is attended by thousands of farm-workers and their families. The bullocks are given several weeks' practice before the event. Two race together in a Roman-style chariot. Bets are wagered on the animals which, despite their bulk, can run surprisingly fast.

Activities for Visitors

Watersports

Surfing is one of the big attractions of Bali. Kuta-Legian's conditions are good for the less experienced surfer. The experts go to Ulu Watu, and the super-confident tackle the shallow reef-break at Padang Padang, just to the north of

there.

Snorkelling. Many of Bali's coastal hotels provide equipment. The best reefs are off Sanur, Candi Dasa and Lovina.

Scuba Diving. The best diving sites are away from the busy tourist areas and require a boat trip to get there. There are clubs offering excursions to the best areas.

Waterskiing is available from Sanur, Kuta, Nusa Dua and Benoa on the coast and, best of all, on Lake Bratan in Central Bali.

Sailing and Windsurfing. Sailing in a native *prahu* is an exciting experience. You go in one of these outrigger fishing boats with the owner.

More conventional sailing is available at watersports clubs in Kuta, Sanur, Nusa Dua and Benoa. **Windsurfing** equipment can also be hired here.

Golf

Bali Handara Golf and Country Club near Lake Bratan – 18-hole, rated among the top 50 courses in the world.

Nusa Dua – 18-hole course.

Tennis

Some of the larger hotels have tennis courts available to non-residents as well as guests. It is advisable to take your own tennis balls.

Climbing

Some of the volcanoes in Central Bali provide a good day's climb (see pages 42 and 51), but there is little to interest the serious climber.

For sports opportunities in Jakarta see page 36.

DIRECTORY

Arriving
The national airline, Garuda
Indonesia, operates daily from
European and North American
airports to Jakarta with onward
connections to Bali. There are
direct flights to Bali from
Australia and New Zealand and
also a few from Europe. It is
difficult to confirm bookings,
and delays are not uncommon;
the flight from London Gatwick
to Soekarno Hatta Airport,
Jakarta, should take 17 hours.
The Dutch airline KLM flies six
times weekly to Jakarta and Bali
from Amsterdam; UTA also has
a regular service from Paris.
Both have connecting flights
from London. Saudia, weekly
outward via Jeddah, is good
value. Shop around for the
cheapest ticket. Book in
advance of Christmas holidays
and the June-September period.

Immigration
Immigration officials are
courteous and efficient, but you
will be sent home if your
passport is not valid for six

*Waves lap against the dark sands of
Ujung's black beach, on the
East Coast*

110

DIRECTORY

months from arrival date. Proof
of onward-return journey is
required. Citizens of UK and
European Community
countries, Australia, New
Zealand, United States and
Canada do not require a visa
for a stay of up to two months if
they are visiting as tourists,
staying in hotel-type
accommodation. This period
cannot be extended without a
visa. Others must obtain a
tourist visa to 30 days from an
Indonesian embassy, or
consulate. Two photographs are
required. All visitors should
acquire a *social visa* if visiting
relatives or friends or a *business
visa*, if on business. Visa
arrangements may alter
suddenly, so check before you
depart.

Airports
Many visitors will arrive at
**Soekarno-Hatta International
Airport**, 14 miles (23km) west
of Jakarta at Tangerang (tel:
5505001/2). Facilities include
bank (open 24 hours);
telephones (collect and credit
card); trolleys and porters; duty
free (expensive and limited);
first aid medical facilities (open
24 hours, vaccinations
available); tourist information
(also offering a hotel reservation
service); left luggage (available
24 hours).
Clean WCs, but uncomfortable
departure lounges. A new
airport will open in the mid-
1990s.
For flight information, call
5505307/8/9. Note that check-in
time is two hours before
departure. An international
airport departure tax is

payable, on both international
and domestic flights (currently
Rp17,000 and Rp5,000
respectively).
Airport buses run every 30
minutes to points in the city
where there are taxi
connections. Your journey into
central Jakarta should take 45
minutes, but rain and traffic jams
often extend it to 60 minutes.
Some hotels provide a bus. Do
not be tricked into taking an air-
conditioned limousine unless
you want to, as it will cost you a
lot more than twice as much as a
taxi and many times the bus fare
(use 'Blue Bird' or 'President'
taxis only). Buses leave Jakarta,
to return to the airport, from
Gambir railway station and
Rawamangun and Blok M bus
stations.

On Bali, **Denpasar (Ngurah Rai)
International Airport** is eight
miles (13km) south of Denpasar;
15 minutes' drive from the city,
20 minutes from Sanur, 15
minutes from Kuta and about an
hour from Ubud. Banking
facilities are open for all flights.
The airport has a hotel bookings
desk. Most major hotels have
meeting services for arriving
guests. Public buses to the city
run every five minutes, except
between about 02.00–04.00 hrs.
Taxis are also available; insist
the driver uses his meter.
Return to the airport by bus is
from Tegal bus station, Jalan
Imam Bonjal.
On departure, check in early.
The departure lounge is
cramped and there is a poor
restaurant/bar and duty-free.
Airport departure tax is payable
as for Jakarta.

Camping
There are no camping-grounds on Bali, as *losmen*/homestays are within every budget. If you really want to 'rough it', then you could: your equipment may be safe, and then again, it may not.

Chemist see Pharmacists

Crime
Sadly, reporting theft has little result in either Jakarta or Bali. Of Jakarta it is said that if you have two sheep and report one stolen to the police, you will find the other gone when you return.

Jakarta
Jakarta has a bad reputation for pickpockets. Areas frequented by tourists are especially vulnerable. Be extra careful around Blok M, and Pasar Baru near the Hotel Melati. A notorious area for robbery is outside Sarinah Department Store; the bus stop here on Jalan MH Thamrin is a major hit-place despite a police office not far away.
If you report a crime, the procedure many take hours.

You can forget the jet-age and travel by pony-trap in Denpasar (it's wise to bargain the fare beforehand)

Virtually no police speak English.

Bali
Robbery is common on Bali, but, conscious of the island's reputation as a tourist resort, police are cracking down. Armed gangs preying on country travellers have been caught, but certain districts remain risky. (See **Personal Safety** page 118.) The worst thieving occurs in Kuta-Legian, but tourists must take some blame. Flaunting valuables, many Australians then complain they were robbed. Often their passport and travellers' cheques disappear from 'under the pillow' when they are drunk. It should be said that crime in Bali, so far only robbery, is not committed by Balinese but by locals from elsewhere in the Indonesian archipelago, and that robbery with violence is rare.

Customs Regulations
The following items, per adult,

DIRECTORY

may be taken duty-free into
Indonesia:
For a **one-week** stay: 200
cigarettes or 50 cigars or 100
grams of tobacco. For a **two-
week** stay: 400 cigarettes or
100 cigars or 200 grams of
tobacco. For a stay **over two-
weeks**: 600 cigarettes or 150
cigars or 300 grams of tobacco;
up to 2 litres of alcohol
(opened); a reasonable amount
of perfume; plus gifts up to a
value of US$100, or equivalent.
Cameras and other
photographic equipment,
televisions, radios, cassette and
video recorders, computers
and typewriters should be
declared on arrival. Prohibited
items include weapons,
ammunition, narcotics and
pornography. Fresh fruits,
plants and animals must have
quarantine permits.
You may not import, or export,
more than Rp50,000. There are
no restrictions on foreign
currency.

Cycling

Cycling is an ideal way of
sightseeing on Bali. The 125-
mile (200km) circle-island tour
via the coast is recommended.
Generally, minor roads are
quiet, but beware of large pot-
holes and some steep hills. To
cope with hills, put your bike on
a *bemo* (see page 121). There
are plenty of rent-a-bicycle
shops in Kuta-Sanur-Ubud.
Finding one that works is a
problem. Rent for a day to test
whether it can manage a longer
journey; then bargain as if your
life depends on it (which it
does). In particular, check the
front and rear brake blocks.

See that the bell works to let
people, poultry and pigs know
you are coming. Dogs are a
nuisance to cyclists. Carry a
minimum of gear. Expect on the
less developed west coast, most
towns with reasonable *losmen*
are within a day's easy ride.
Repairs are not expensive.
Wear a hat and cover exposed
arms and legs with sunblock to
protect yourself.

Driving

In Jakarta
No foreigner tackles self-drive
in Jakarta. Hertz and Avis
operate chauffeur-driven
limousines:
Hertz: tel: 332610/332739;
Avis: tel: 331974/332900.

On Bali
What Bali earns from tourism
does not equate with central
government spending on roads.
There is a two-lane motorway
between Denpasar and Benoa.
Elsewhere, roads are badly pot-
holed and secondary roads
may be tracks. Any sort of self-
drive requires considerable
skill. Experience of driving in
Asia is useful. Denpasar is best
avoided: the narrow streets are
choked with buses, cars and
motorbikes. If you stay
somewhere such as Kuta or
Candi Dasa, renting a bicycle is
recommended (see **Cycling**).
Rent a Suzuki, for longer trips
away from base.
Self-drive is ideal for three to
four companions. Even if you
are on your own, it is
remarkably cheap. You require
an **international driving
licence** (available from major
motoring organisations in your

own country). Driving is on the left. Pull well over for the long distance Denpasar–Jakarta buses, which are recklessly driven. Avoid as far as possible the Denpasar–Gianyar–Klungkung road at peak times. The amount of traffic unfortunately makes any time seem like rush-hour in Bali. Only on the rough, rural roads can you relax baring pot-holes. Roads are well signposted.
Petrol stations on the other hand are few and far between. When you see one, fill your tank. You can see Bali easily in a week's self-drive. Chauffeurs are available from most rent-a-car companies. **Car rental** on Bali really means jeep-rental. The most popular vehicles for hire are Suzuki, Jimmy and open-top VW safari. The Suzuki is ideal. Shopping around for a good deal is dubious and it is better to pay more to get a reliable car. There are numerous car-rental agencies in Kuta and Denpasar and in Sanur and Ubud, but your hotel should be able to make arrangements for you.
Motorcycles. There are frightful motorcycle accidents in Bali. Bad roads are mainly to blame. Although it is hot, wear long trousers in case you skid and suffer 'gravel rash'. Pack mercurochrome or other astringent, and equip yourself for cool, wet weather in the mountains.
Most bikes range between 90 and 125cc. You do not need anything faster. If you do not have an international driving licence, endorsed for a motorcycle, you will need a temporary motorcycle licence

A flying masterpiece: kites can be works of art as well as great fun

valid for one month for Bali. Arranged by the bike's owner, this means a trip to Denpasar. Allow four to five hours to be photographed and fingerprinted, to pass a simple written exam and take a riding test.
Rental charges vary according to the bike, the owner and how long you want it. Shop around. Everyone in Kuta seems to have a bike for hire. Check it thoroughly, and be prepared to pay for something decent. Girls who wish to see Bali on a motorbike can hire a driver for a couple of thousand *rupiah* extra. It also saves paying compulsory insurance. Punctures are a common occurrence; fortunately you will rarely be far from someone who can fix it for you (look for signs saying 'Presban', 'Servis' or 'Bengkel').

Drugs
Indonesia does not have a serious local drug problem. The

DIRECTORY

fate of foreigners found in possession of drugs varies from immediate deportation to authorities in their country of origin to a jail sentence. Indonesian law requires you to report drug offenders, or face arrest yourself. Without cash, you may remain inside some time.

Electricity

Most hotels use 220 volts 50 cycles, though some hotels and *losmen* in outlying districts may use 110 volts. Electrical appliances without dual voltage may require a voltage transformer. Sockets accept two-round-pronged plugs. For most Western visitors, an electrical adaptor is needed.

Embassies and Consulates

Embassies
Australia: Jalan MH Thamrin 15, Jakarta (tel: 323109)
Canada: Wisma Metropolitan Building 1, 5th floor, Jalan Jend Sudirman 29, Jakarta (tel: 510709)

Great Britain: Jalan MH Thamrin 75, Jakarta (tel: 330904)
New Zealand: Jalan Diponegoro 41, Jakarta (tel: 330552)
US: Jalan Merdeka Selatan 5, Jakarta (tel: 360360)

Consulates and Foreign Representatives on Bali
There is no British consulate on Bali, but the Australian Consulate handles the affairs of British citizens, plus those of Canadians and New Zealanders.
Australian Consulate, Jalan Raya Sanur 146, Tanjung Bungkak, Denpasar (tel: 25997/8)
Consular Agency of the United States of America, Jalan Segara Ayu 5, Sanur (tel: 88478). Open 08.00–14.00 hrs Monday to Friday, but a consular representative is available 24 hours for emergencies.

Balinese artistry is everywhere

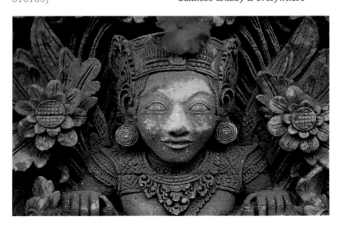

Emergency Telephone Numbers

Police 110
Fire 113
Ambulance 118

Jakarta Hospitals
RS Aini, Jalan HR Rasuna Said Kuningan (tel: 516109)
RS Auri, Jalan Kesehatan IV/26 (tel: 342940)
RS Unika Atmajaya, Jalan Pluit Raya 2 (tel: 661909)

Bali Police
Jalan Diponegoro, Denpasar (tel: 110)
Jalan Ray Kuta, Kuta (tel: 51598)

Bali Hospitals/Clinics
Sanglah Public Hospital, Jalan Kesehatan 1, Sanglah Denpasar (tel: (0361) 27911)
Wangaya Public Hospital, Jalan Kartini, Denpasar (tel: (0361) 22141)
Emergency Dental Treatment, Dr Indra Guizot, Jalan Pattimura 19, Denpasar (tel: 22445, 26445)
Surya Husadha Clinic, Jalan Pulau Serangan 1-3, Denpasar (tel: 25249). This private hospital is specially geared to tourists. It offers insurance cover for your stay on the island.

Entertainment Information

For current information on entertainment in Jakarta, consult the *Jakarta Post's* 'What's On' section or *Guide to Jakarta* tourist magazine (free in travel agencies and hotels). The English-language paper *Indonesian Times* has a 'Where To Go' section (also for Bali).

Health

No health regulations apply in Indonesia, except inoculation against yellow fever if coming from an infected zone.

Visiting Jakarta and Bali can be medically safe if you take precautions. This applies mainly to what you eat and drink and how much you expose yourself to sun. Take it easy for 48 hours after you arrive. Jet-lag changes your sleeping and eating patterns and your body is most vulnerable to climatic changes at this time. No special medications are required; both Jakarta and Bali are malaria free although the tourist office do recommend that you take Malaria tablets, as well as typhoid and cholera injections, as a precaution. It is also advisable to have a tetanus injection before your visit. Mosquitoes are a menace, so equip yourself with a good repellent. Most non-air-conditioned hotels supply coils, or spray your room. Adhere to the following basic rules and you will, with luck, remain healthy.

Wear a hat, sunglasses and high protection sunscreen (Factor 15+).

If you sweat profusely, you may need to **take salt-tablets**.

Drink plenty. Local water is unsafe, but good, cheap bottled water is sold everywhere. If you cannot obtain any, drink fresh coconut juice. Local beer is a good thirst-quencher in the tropics.

Do not over-indulge. Drinking plus eating plus sun often equals upset stomach. Usually non-infectious, diarrhoea often results from this combination, or from eating hot, unfamiliar, spicy dishes. Plain boiled rice,

DIRECTORY

Herbal medicine on sale in the Sarinah Department Store, Jakarta

or *bubur* (rice cooked in stock with vegetables) is recommended while the stomach is recovering. Carry anti-diarrhoeal tablets and avoid ice cubes. Most hotels know the dangers of contaminated water and supply jugs of boiled water, but drop a water-purifying tablet in to be sure. Gastro-intestinal diseases can be picked up anywhere, but they are less likely to be encountered in a de luxe hotel, a *warung* where locals eat, or Chinese restaurants where food is freshly prepared. Second-grade hotels with sub-standard cooking and hygiene arrangements are often suspect. Food cooked in the streets – bananas, sweet potato, etc – is generally safe. Check the cooking oil is clean and buy only freshly cooked food, not from a ready-cooked pile. Except in specialised food outlets, eating yoghurt or ice-cream is risky.

Doctors (Doktor)
Ask your hotel (if staying in a cheap *losmen*, contact an international hotel and ask the concierge) to recommend a doctor, or call your embassy, or the European manager of your airline. A Chinese doctor is preferable. Jakarta has the best medical services. Only a hospital, not a clinic, will take an emergency case. If seriously ill, fly home. Bali has a poor reputation for health services, although there is a special ward for tourists in the main hospital in Denpasar. (See **Emergency Telephone Numbers** page 115 for hospitals.)

Medical Treatments
Jamu are cheap, traditional medicines made from plants, minerals and animals. You can recognise a *jamu* stall by the shelves of little jars and packets. Find someone who can translate your problem – the vendor will have precisely what you need… and it may cure you!
Sarinah Department Store in Jakarta has a traditional medicine counter in the basement. If you want something for a cold, flu or a sprain, 'Silver Clove' medicated balm, Balsam Cengkeh 10 is excellent.
See also **Pharmacists**.

Take out adequate travel insurance, including a provision to get 'medi-vacced' by air-ambulance if necessary.

Holidays, public
1 January: New Year's Day is observed throughout the

country.
21 April: Kartini Day
17 August: Proklomasi Kemerdekaan (Independence Day)
5 October: Armed Forces Day
25 December: Christmas Day
In addition, there are the Muslim religious festivals of *lebaran* and *Grebeg Besar* and the Chinese New Year celebrations (all based on the lunar calendar); the Balinese New Year (Nyepi) in March/ April; and Good Friday and Ascension Day, celebrated by Christians.
(See also **Special Events** pages 105–107).

Money Matters

The Indonesian unit of currency is the *rupiah*, which comes in the following denominations: bill/banknotes: Rp100, Rp500, Rp1,000, Rp5,000, Rp10,000, coins: Rp5, Rp10, Rp25, Rp50, Rp100.
It is a good plan to have sufficient *rupiah* in smaller denominations (Rp50, Rp100), as many taxi drivers and small stores may not have small change. It is also advisable to take enough *rupiah* when travelling outside major tourist destinations. Daily exchange rates are posted at banks and in leading daily newspapers. In Indonesia, money-changers give a better rate than hotels. Banks in Jakarta give a better rate of exchange than in outlying areas. Shop around. Travellers' cheques can usually be cashed at hotels, banks and money-changers.
Credit cards are widely accepted in Jakarta and popular tourist resorts in Bali. Use Visa, Diners Club and American Express for preference.
Banking hours are from 07.30/08.00 to 12.30/13.00 hrs (and for a time in the afternoon), Mondays to Fridays; and from 08.00 to 12.00/13.00 hrs on Saturdays. Cash desks in banks may not be open in the afternoons and will also close at least one hour before the bank closes.

Opening Times
Government offices in Indonesia generally open from 08.00 to 15.00 hrs from Monday to Thursday; from 08.00 to 11.30 hrs on Friday and from 08.00 to 14.00 hrs on Saturday.
Business offices have varied hours. Some open from 08.00 to 16.00, others from 09.00 to 17.00 hrs. Other offices work half day on Saturdays; some are closed.
Banks open from 07.30 or 08.00 hrs to about 16.00 hrs. Most banks are also open Saturday mornings. Cash desks close at least one hour before the bank closes. Money-changers stay open till evening.
Indonesians like to complete most work before the midday heat. The best time to make appointments is between 08.00 and 11.00 hrs.

On Bali, government offices are open from 08.00 to 14.00 hrs Monday to Thursday, on Fridays until 11.00 hrs, and some Saturdays until 12.30 hrs. Most shops, stores and shopping-centres are open six days a week, from 08.00 to 15.00 hrs and from 17.00 to 20.00 hrs in the evening, except on public holidays. Some shops open on Sundays.

DIRECTORY

Personal Safety

Crime against the person is rare in Indonesia, but theft is something to guard against. In Jakarta, expect to be robbed if you travel on local buses. Thieves – often from Sumatra – work in gangs. One, perhaps a girl, will distract you with a pleasantry. Once your gaze is averted, the gang will strike. It is unlikely you can react as the culprit melts into the crowd. Never carry your airline ticket, passport or more money than necessary. If shopping, a credit card in a buttoned-up breast pocket is ideal. Be alert. Avoid walking about after dark. Ignore anyone slowing down in a car, or *bejaj* (see page 121). On Bali, the Lake Batur area is crime-prone. Be careful of your bag, camera, pocket. Do not leave a rented vehicle without a companion to guard it. It may not start when you return. Do not engage in conversation in this area. The people are different from on the coast. The Kintamani-Bangli region is dubious, but as with everything, it all depends who is up to no good when you are there. In the coastal resorts, take nothing to the beach unless someone you know can watch it while you swim. Enquire if your hotel, or *losmen* has a security box. The money-changer at 'Bemo Corner' in Kuta has safe-deposit facilities. Be careful of mini-buses, *bemos* and *bejaj* which stop without being hailed. Also, on crowded *bemos* beware of smiling faces offering assistance by taking your luggage and placing it at the far end of the compartment, do not be surprised if your bag feels lighter at the end of the journey. Ideally try to travel with Balinese women and children.

Pharmacists

You can obtain most drugs – analgesics, antibiotics, vitamins, etc – from local pharmacists (*apotik*). A prescription is unnecessary. Bargain in smaller pharmacies.
Most medications are expensive, so make up a small kit from home: water purifying tablets, aspirin or other pain-killer, anti-diarrhoeal tablets, vitamin C, lip-balm, Dettol/astringent, first aid dressings, decongestant, etc.

Photography

Indonesia, especially Bali, is one of the most photogenic places on earth. Most people do not object to being photographed but if they do, desist. Anyone connected with the tourist trade may require payment. You should oblige with a small sum if the photo is important. Photography shops in Kuta-Legian and Sanur on Bali develop prints rapidly and usually well. Jalan Agus Salim is where to develop and buy film in Jakarta; also for cameras. Slow speed film is okay for the coast. You will need faster – 100 ASA – in misty mountain areas. A flash is useful, but should not be used when photographing temple ceremonies. Never leave your camera in a bus as the heat will destroy the film. A plastic bag protects your camera in sudden showers. Museums in Jakarta charge for photography (Rp500 for still cameras, Rp1,000 for videos).

The beauty of a Balinese temple pond. Religion dominates life here

Places of Worship

In Jakarta, the **Gereja Immanuel** at Jalan Merdeka Timur has Protestant Sunday services in Dutch and English. The following Christian services are held on Bali:

Holy Mass
Denpasar: St Joseph Church, Kepundung – Saturday, 17.30 hrs. Sunday, 07.00, 08.30 and 17.30 hrs.
Hotel Bali Beach, Sanur, Legong Room – Saturday, 18.00 hrs (in English).
Hotel Bali Hyatt, Sanur: Hibiscus Room – Saturday, 19.00 hrs (in English).
Nusa Dua Beach Hotel: Garuda Room – Sunday, 18.00 hrs (in English).
Hotel Melia Bali Sol, Nusa Dua: Bali Room – Sunday, 18.00 hrs (in English)
Kuta: St Francis Xavier Church – Saturday, 18.00 hrs. Sunday, 08.00 hrs.

Protestant Services
Denpasar: Maranatha Church, Surapati – Sunday, 09.00 and 18.00 hrs.
Gereja Kirsten Protestan di Bali, Jalan Debes – Sunday 07.00, 09.00 and 18.00 hrs.
Hotel Bali Beach, Sanur: Legong Room – Sunday, 18.00 hrs (in English).
Hotel Putra Bali, Nusa Dua: Bale Ubud – Sunday, 17.30 hrs (in English).

Police see Crime

Post Office

Most hotels in Jakarta provide postal services. If you prefer to mail your letter, the following are some post addresses:
Central Post Office, Jalan Pos Utara 2, Pasar Baru (tel: 350004)
Gajahmada Post Office, Jalan Gajahmada (tel: 346595)
Jakarta Kota Post Office, Jalan Fatahillah 3 (tel: 679800).

Post Office addresses on Bali are:
Denpasar: Central Post Office, Jalan Raya Puputan, Renon
Sanur: Banjar Taman, Sanur
Kuta: Jalan Ray Tuban, Kuta
Ubud: Banjar Taman, Ubud
Singaraja: Jalan Gajahmada, Singaraja
All offer poste restante.

Public Transport

Inter-island Travel
Inter-island travel is effected by regular air services of Garuda Indonesia and its subsidiary Merpati using B737, DC-9, F28 and A300 airbus. Other airlines offering domestic flights are Bouraq, Mandala, Sempati, Seulawah and Zamrud. Scheduled ferry sailings and

DIRECTORY

irregular departures by *bugis* schooners make up a miraculously good overall communications network. Addresses in Jakarta of Garuda Indonesia and other domestic airlines are:

Garuda Indonesia, BDN Building, Jalan MH Thamrin 5, (tel: 334425, 334429, 334430, 334434)

Bouraq Indonesia Airlines, Jalan Angkasa, 1–3 Kemayoran (tel: 6595194, 6595179)

Mandala Airlines, Jalan Veteran 1/34 (tel: 368107)

Merpati Nusantara Airlines, Jalan Angkasa, 2 Kemayoran (tel: 417404, 413608)

Pelita Air Service, Jalan Abdul Muis 52-54 (tel: 375908)

Huge pinisis *ply between islands in the Indonesian archipelago*

Sempati Air Transport, Jalan Merdeka Timur 7 (tel: 348760, 343323)

Addresses of airline offices on Bali are:

Garuda Indonesia: Jalan Melati 61, Denpasar (tel: 22788/34606)

Bouraq Indonesia Airlines: Jalan Sudirman 19A, Denpasar (tel: 24656)

Merpati Nusantara: Jalan Melati 57, Denpasar (tel: 22864/25841).

Visitors can travel from Jakarta by rail to all the major cities and towns in Java and to towns in the southern part of Sumatra via Merak. For connections with Bali, the State Railways offer a combination bus/train ticket from Bali to Jakarta, but not the other way round.

Denpasar is the main travel terminus on Bali. Boat, train and plain tickets are sold here. For travel to Jakarta, Lorena Continental overland bus is recommended. It has air conditioning, WC, videos. Travelling time from Denpasar to Jakarta is 1½ days. Fare includes snacks and a lunch.

Getting About Jakarta

Buses: Some 20 bus companies operate all over Jakarta. They are cheap, crowded and difficult to board. If you take a bus, sit at the front and beware of pickpockets. **Be alert for thieves at a bus-stop.** Avoid Jakarta rush-hour between 07.30–08.30 and 16.00–17.30 hrs. Mini-buses, or *oplets* (slightly more expensive) are safer, with seated passengers only.

Bus Terminals are at Gambir

Railway Station; Jalan Bulungan, Blok M Kemayoran Baru; Kemayoran; Rawamangun; Pasar Minggu; and Halim Perdana Kusuma.

See under Arriving for services to Jakarta's main airport. There is also a regular bus shuttle serving the city's second airport, Halim Perdana Kusuma.

Bejaj: These noisy rattle-traps are motorised three-wheel taxis, often the quickest way to commute. Take a scarf to shield your face from the fumes as locals do. Bargain the fare; if this is disputed by the driver, wave him on and wait for another. A chartered *bejaj* between three companions is a good plan for sightseeing. Learn where you wish to go in Indonesian as the driver will not speak English. *Bejaj* are found all over the city.

Taxis: Beware of private taxis. Avoid yellow cabs. Take only Bluebird and President.
Bluebird: tel: 325607 (blue)
President: tel: 4895978 (yellow/red).
Taxis have a special hourly rate for sightseeing trips.

Getting About Bali

Buses: Buses cover the main 'inter-town' routes, with Denpasar as the central terminal. In addition, all main routes, as well as minor passable ones are covered by *Colts* and *bemos* (see below).

Bemos: This is the most popular means of transport. The Bali version of the *bejaj*, it is a small, noisy three-wheel motorbike-taxi, driven recklessly in and out of traffic-jams. Most operate a standard route, picking up and depositing passengers along the way. *Bemo* drivers have a price for locals and another price for tourists. Ask Balinese travellers what they pay. Beware of pickpockets on popular tourist routes such as Kuta-Legian-Denpasar-Ubud. A fun idea is to charter a *bemo* for a day, or longer. Pick a good one. Regular *bemos* can squeeze in 12 people. Do not get into a *bemo* with three, or four apparently friendly young men. An unfortunate sign of the times is that they might rob you. (See **Personal Safety** page 118). There are four main bus and *bemo* terminals in Denpasar: Ubung (serving the west and north of Bali); Kereneng (the east); Tegal (services Kuta and Nusa Dua); and Wangaya (a route north via Sangeh). Another small bus station, Suci, serves points south, including Benoa Port.

Colts: the name comes from Mitsubishi Colt mini-buses but any small bus is known as a 'Colt'. They are marginally more expensive than a larger bus, but are more comfortable. They ply everywhere on Bali. See also **Cycling** and **Driving**.

Senior Citizens

Indonesia is not suitable for elderly tourists unless they are especially fit and able to cope with the heat. Bali's rough roads and temple stairways are very taxing.

Student and Youth Travel

Indonesia is ideal for youth travel. If offers bargain-priced adventure. Student-cards are recognised by many places. Bali is in particular geared to young visitors and many may find the surf, shops and bars in Kuta ideal.

Telephones

Indonesia's own satellite offers efficient communications overseas. Direct dialling is available in major hotels which may not charge more than 10 per cent on top of operator calls. However, it is cheaper in major cities like Jakarta and Denpasar to dial from the city telephone office (Kantor Telekommunikasi). There are collect and credit card telephones in the departure lounges of Soekarno Hatta and Denpasar airports.

To telephone to the UK from Indonesia, dial 0044, then the local STD code (minus the first 0) and the customer number. For operator assistance in making your international call, dial 101 or, in Jakarta, 104. The dialling code for Indonesia from abroad is 01062, plus 21 for Jakarta and 361 for Denpasar.

Time

Indonesia is divided into three time zones. Western Indonesia Standard Time (including Sumatra, **Java**, West Kalimantan, Central Kalimantan) is seven hours ahead of Greenwich Mean Time (GMT); Central Indonesia Standard Time (East Kalimantan, South Kalimantan, **Bali**, Sulawesi, Nusatenggara) is eight hours ahead; and Eastern Indonesia Standard Time, which covers Irian Jaya and the Maluku islands, is nine hours ahead of GMT.

Thus for most of the year, when it is 12 noon in Bali it is 04.00 hrs

The stillness of the lakes near Bedugal, in Bali's Central Mountains

in London; 23.00 hrs (the previous day) in New York and Montreal; 14.00 hrs in Sydney; and 16.00 hrs in New Zealand. When it is 12 noon in Jakarta it is 05.00 hrs in London; 12 midnight in New York and Montreal; 15.00 hrs in Sydney; and 17.00 hrs in New Zealand.

Tipping

Tipping is not traditional in Indonesia, but there are certain charges for services such as airport porterage. Leading hotels and restaurants add 10 per cent service to bills. Where they do not, a 10–15 per cent tip is now customary. Porters and others who perform services are often grateful for a small tip of Rp500-1,000. Leave taxi drivers small change. Do not, however, insist on giving anyone a tip, as many Balinese look on tipping as charity and find it humiliating.

Toilets and Washing Facilities

All tourist hotels have western-style WCs. Elsewhere are squat lavatories, flushed by water from a dipper which floats in a tub of water by the toilet, or a tap. Water from the dipper is used by Indonesians to cleanse themselves. It is advisable to carry a supply of paper. A bin is often provided for soiled material, which would block the system. There are next to no public WCs although they are always installed in museums. If you need a lavatory, go into a hotel or café. The better the establishment, the better the WC.

Cheaper hotels and *losmen* have Indonesian-style bathrooms, or *mandi*, with tiled floors and a tub which you fill with water. Do not sit in the tub as you might get stuck. Stand beside it and pour water over yourself with the plastic dipper, or *gajung*. Hot water is rare in cheap establishments; you may miss it in mountain areas. For that reason, take a *mandi* around 17.00 hours, before the evening chill sets in.

Tourist Offices

One of the main reasons why Indonesia is not better known as a tourist destination is the dearth of tourist promotion offices abroad.

United Kingdom/Eire, Benelux and Scandinavia

Indonesian Tourist Promotion Office, 3–4 Hanover Street, London W1 9HH (tel: (071) 493 0030/493 0334).

The **Indonesian Embassy**, 38 Grosvenor Square, London W1X 9AD (tel: (071) 499 7661), may be able to help with certain enquiries.

Germany

Indonesia Tourist Promotion Offices, Wiessenhutten Strasse, 17, D6000, Frankfurt-am-Main (tel: (069) 233677/233678).

North America

Indonesia Tourist Promotion Offices, 3457 Wilshire Boulevard, Los Angeles, CA 90010, USA (tel: (213) 3872078).

Australia

Indonesia Tourist Promotion, Level 10, 5 Elizabeth Street, Sydney, NSW 2000 (tel: (02) 233360).

Tourist Information Offices in Jakarta:

Visitor Information Centres

Jakarta Theatre Building, Jalan MH Thamrin 9, Jakarta Pusat 10340 (tel: 354094; 364093). Oriental Building, Jalan MH Thamrin 51, Jakarta Pusat 10350 (tel: 332067)

Visitor Information Service

Jakarta International Airport, Soekarno-Hatta Cengkareng, Jakarta Barat 19110 (tel: 5507088)

Jakarta Metropolitan City Tourism Development Board

Jalan KH Abdul Rohim 2, Kuningan Barat, Jakarta Selatan 12710 (tel: 511073, 511369, 510738).

Tourist Information Offices on Bali:

Diparda Tk 1 Bali

Jalan S. Parman, Niti Mandala

(tel: (0361) 22387/26313).

Bali Government Tourist Office
Jalan Raya Pupatan, Renon, Denpasar (Sanur exit) (tel: (0361) 25649).

Badung Government Tourist Office (Badung District)
Jalan Surapati 7, Denpasar (near central museum), tel: (0361) 23602/23399.
Open: 08.00–14.00 hrs (until 11.00 hrs Friday and 12.30 hrs Saturday). Closed Sunday. Tourist information offices are also found in Gianyar, Ubud, Singaraja and Kuta.

Travel Agencies
There are countless tour operators offering a variety of tour programmes on Bali. Most agencies are in Denpasar, Kuta-Legian and Sanur. Compare prices. If you can, check with someone who has done a tour. Some tour programmes pack too much into eight to nine hours' drive – remember Bali's roads are rough and busy.

Oriental grace: the water palace complex of Tirtagangga

Major operators include:
Bianglala Tours & Travel: Jalan By-Pass Ngurah Rai 50, Sanur (tel: (0361) 87710).
Bali Indonesia Murni Tour & Travel: Jalan Semawang, Sanur (tel: (0361) 88463).
Pacto Ltd: Jalan By-Pass Ngurah Rai, Sanur (tel: (0361) 87135).
Santa Bali Tours & Travel: Hotel Bali Beach, Sanur (tel: (0361) 87628).
Surya Permata Tours & Travel: Jalan Melasti Legian, Kuta (tel: (0361) 51673).
Wisata Dewa Tours & Travel: Jalan Diponegro No. 98, Blok C-3, Denpasar (tel: (0361) 37680).

If you make only one tour, visit **Ubud-Mas** and **Bedugal-Lake Bratan**. The eight hour tour to **Kintamani** visiting Lake Batur and stopping in Celuk, Mas, Ubud and Tampaksiring is also recommended.

For travel agencies in Jakarta see page 19.

LANGUAGE

More than 250 languages and dialects are spoken in Indonesia, but the lingua franca is *Bahasa Indonesia*, spoken by the majority. In Jakarta one in ten people also speaks some English. Balinese is altogether different. It has a different vocabulary and conversation is complicated by caste, depending to whom you are speaking (see page 103). Concentrate on *Bahasa Indonesia*: it makes travel easier and people are delighted to be addressed in their own language. *Pasar* or 'market' Indonesian is a simplified, colloquial form. Similar to Malay, *Bahasa Indonesia* has no complex rules, nor the tonal complications that make Asian languages difficult.

Grammar

Indonesian has no articles, genders or cases; conjunctions are likewise unknown. To form the plural, double the noun, eg suitcase – *kopor*, suitcases *kopor kopor*. An adjective is always placed after the noun. To make a question of a sentence, simply raise the pitch of your voice at the end of the phrase. Indonesian is phonetic. Most consonants sound like English consonants. Vowels are more confusing: pronounce 'a' like the 'u' in 'up' – eg *apa kabar* (how are you?); 'e' is a short sound not always pronounced, eg *selamat datang* (welcome) becomes *slamat datang*. Indonesian is written in Latin characters adapted from an early Arabic version, using 21 letters of the alphabet. Remember that each single letter represents a sound. Below are some useful words and phrases:

Basics

I, my and mine saya
no tidak
yes ya
he, she, it/his, her, its dia
good bagus
you kamu
we (including the person addressed) kita
we (not including the person addressed) kami
they mereka
big besar
small kecil
welcome selamat datang
good morning (until 11.00 hrs) selamat pagi
good afternoon (11.00–15.00 hrs) selamat siang
good afternoon (15.00 hrs to nightfall) selamat sore
good evening selamat malam
good night selamat tidur
enjoy your meal selamat makan
thank you terima kasih
excuse me ma'af permisi
how are you? apa kabar?
goodbye sampai bertemu lagi
what is that? apaka itu?
do you speak English? saudara bicara bahasa Inggris?
I don't understand saya tidak mengerti
I would like saya minta

Directions

where dimana
from dari
to ke
here kemana
there demana
straight ahead terus
stop berhenti
north utara

south selatan
east timur
west barat
left kiri
right kanan
near dekat
far jauh
direction jurusan
down/below bawah
up/above atas

Numbers

1 satu
2 dua
3 tiga
4 empat
5 lima
6 enam
7 tujuh
8 delapan
9 sembilan
10 sepuluh
11 sebelas
12 duabelas
13 tigabelas
20 dua puluh
30 tiga puluh
100 seratus
1000 seribu
2000 duaribu
10,000 sepuluh ribu
100,000 seratus ribu
500,000 lima ratus
1 million satu juta

Food

Makan is both the verb 'to eat' and
the noun 'food'. A restaurant is
therefore *rumah makan*, or 'house
food'. Below are some basic items
of food and drink:
bread roti
sweets gula-gula
egg telur
chilli lombok
ginger jahe
salt garam
pepper merika
sugar gula
fish ikan

oysters tiram
crab kepiting
prawn udang
shrimp undang kecil

Vegetables
cucumber mentimun
beans buncis
onion bawang
potato kentang

Drinks
beer bir
boiled water air putih
orange/lemon juice air jeruk/air
    jeruk nipis
coffee kopi
milk susu
rice wine brem
tea teh
May we have our bill please?
    Coba berikan rekening saya?

In the Restaurant
The following words will help you
to read the menu:
nasi putih plain white rice
nasi goreng fried rice with
ancillaries such as fried egg,
chicken, peppers etc, but usually
meaning fried rice
nasi sayur rice with vegetables
nasi campur rice with a selection
of things including meat
nasi padang rice with spicy side-
dishes
mie kuah noodle soup
babi guling roast baby pig
betutu bebek steamed duck
gado-gado cold cooked
vegetable salad (lettuce,
cucumber, tomato, hard-boiled
egg, etc) with peanut sauce
saté chicken or lamb barbecued
on skewers and eaten with peanut
dip
cap cai vegetable or meat chop
suey
rijstaffel a selection of
Indonesian dishes of Dutch
colonial tradition

INDEX

The Automobile Association would like to thank the following photographers and libraries for their assistance in the preparation of this book.

CHRISTINE OSBORNE took all the photographs in this book except those listed below (© AA Photo Library).

NATURE PHOTOGRAPHERS LTD 78 Lar gibbon, 79 Leaf insect (S C Bisserot), 80 Black drongo (M Hill), 83 Tree ferns (K J Carlson), 84 Atlas beetle, 84 Blue-tailed banded pitta (S C Bisserot).

SPECTRUM COLOUR LIBRARY Cover Traditional Dance.

Author's Acknowledgements
The author would like to thank the following for help in the updating of this guide:
Directorate General of Tourism, Jakarta; Grand Hyatt Jakarta, Sobek Expeditions, Bali and Sempati Air.

For this revision: Copy editor Jenny Fry
Thanks also to Christine Osborne for her updating work on this revised edition.